STRONGER

Forty Days
of Metal and
Spirituality

STRONGER

BRIAN "HEAD" WELCH

WITH ILLUSTRATIONS BY JOSHUA CLAY

HarperOne
An Imprint of HarperCollinsPublishers

HarperOne

STRONGER: *Forty Days of Metal and Spirituality.* Copyright © 2010 by Brian Welch. All rights reserved. Printed in the United States of America. No part of this book may be used or reproduced in any manner whatsoever without written permission except in the case of brief quotations embodied in critical articles and reviews. For information address HarperCollins Publishers, 10 East 53rd Street, New York, NY 10022.

HarperCollins books may be purchased for educational, business, or sales promotional use. For information please write: Special Markets Department, HarperCollins Publishers, 10 East 53rd Street, New York, NY 10022.

FIRST EDITION

Designed by Ralph Fowler
Illustrations by Joshua Clay

Library of Congress Cataloging-in-Publication Data is available upon request.

ISBN 978–0–06–155582–4

10 11 12 13 14   RRD(H)   10 9 8 7 6 5 4 3 2 1

This book is dedicated to everyone who reads it. Life is a war, man, but every battle we face can be used as a tool to make us stronger.

STRONGER

INTRODUCTION

N JANUARY 2005 I found God, and I've never been the same since. For years before that life-changing decision, I had been the lead guitarist for the band Korn, traveling the world and making millions of dollars, all while being hopelessly addicted to crystal meth. I had a daughter I was responsible for, and I was failing her. I had a life I was throwing away, and I woke up each day wishing that some force would simply take me out of my misery. Thankfully that didn't happen. Instead of that force taking me out of my misery, I got a new reason to live.

That was five years ago, and looking back on it now, I'm amazed at the distance that I've traveled. When I think back to the man I used to be, I'm completely tripped out about how beaten up and defeated I was. On the outside, I was living like a king, with all the power in my hands to do whatever I wanted, as well as order *others* to do what I wanted them to do for me. But on the inside I was a scared, weak little boy who was screaming and wailing as hard and loud as I could for help. But no one could hear me because I was afraid to let my cries be heard on the outside, to let the truth be told, to show my weakness. Simply put, I was scared to admit that I was a failure when, on the outside, I looked like such a success. I couldn't tell the truth that I, a person with so much power and success, needed help.

The exterior of a person reveals only so much. When you look at someone, what you see on the surface is not the true image of that person. The real story lies beneath the skin. That's where the person's true life is lived—in that secret inner sanctum where every human being resides. That space, invisible to everyone else, is where true strength and character begin if we let them, but so many of us spend our time behind our masks and never develop that inner strength.

Before I found God, that was how I lived, until I became so disgusted with hiding that I decided to tell the truth to everyone about the person I'd become.

I decided to let my cries for help be heard.

After I finally made that incredibly important decision, I came to realize the most valuable lesson that a person can learn on earth: my failure in life and my willingness to surrender were the keys that opened the door to a whole new existence. As I faced my weakness and failure head on, I suddenly saw that I was in the perfect place to receive the strength that I didn't have—a strength that could come only from divine love. So I decided to make God the love of my life from that day on. That love picked me up, cleansed me, healed me, and cared for me. We all have the desire to be passionately treasured and loved. We get that desire from God, because all that God desires from us is to be passionately treasured and loved.

When that door to God's love had been opened, I became hungry to explore his love as much as possible. I'm no brainiac, but I figured that one of the best ways to learn how to love God was through the Bible. I was right: from that book, I learned a lot about what God loves and what He dislikes. Perhaps even more amazing was that, as I read through the Bible, I felt like I wasn't reading it alone. I felt like God's Spirit was right there reading it with me, teaching me things about divine love. That feeling of companionship is still there now, every time I pick up the book, and I'm sure it feels like that because it's actually true.

Today I'm stronger than I've ever been in my life, capable of facing any challenge that comes at me, and my experiences with the Bible have a lot to do with that. But it's been a long, hard road to get here. Even now I still have my bad days—times when I struggle with anger and sadness. But deep inside of me there's a stillness that never goes away. It's a calm that always lives in me, no matter what else is going on—a calm that only I can see—and there isn't a storm that will ever disturb that ocean of peace.

The Bible injects life into that calm, fueling it at all times. I decided to put this book together because I wanted to share some of the things I've learned from the Bible about divine love. I chose forty of my favorite scripture passages, one for each "day" of this book, because it seemed like a good number. I quote the passage and then offer some thoughts on how that particular scripture has touched my life. My thought is that you will read the book a "day" at a time, giving you time to meditate on each scripture passage and digest my take on it.

Now, I've said it before and I'll say it again. I know how it feels for people who don't really believe in God to hear someone else talk about Him. You kind of roll your eyes and think to yourself, "Okay, here comes the crazy talk." But if that's you, just keep on reading, because those feelings will start to go away. I talk about a lot of other things in this book, too. Trust me: you can handle it.

Sharing scripture was a big part of why I wanted to write the book, but there's another reason. My journey with faith has been just that—a journey. I've had highs and lows, and I've experienced other crazy things that I want to share. Because through it all, I've had God at my side. I'll be the first one to admit that I'm a pretty odd nut job sometimes, so this will not be your typical devotional book. I'm proud to be unique, and I encourage others to do the same. Who wants to be like everyone else?

Not me.

If you're reading this book only to hear more insane stories about my rock star life, that's cool with me. But my main prayer is that you experience divine love as you read this, because you are *not* reading it alone. Just as God's Spirit is with me when I read the Bible, He is right there reading this book with you. It may sound crazy to some of you, but it's true. So sit back, relax, and let's go on a forty-day journey together.

—Head

DAY 1

Matthew 16:26

And what do you benefit if you gain the whole world but lose your own soul? Is anything worth more than your soul?

IN THE YEAR 2000, back when I was still with Korn, I was given some news that completely rocked my world. My manager called and told me that Korn was going on tour with Metallica, Kid Rock, and System of a Down. That was a dream-come-true tour for me. Everyone in the metal community respected Metallica as pioneers in inventing dark, melodic metal. They had influenced so many great bands over the years. I never got into Kid Rock, but I thought he had some cool songs and I'd heard nothing but great things about him. His reputation was that he *loved* to party (as much as ten rock stars, it was said) and had no "I'm better than you" attitude at all. System of a Down was pretty new to the scene back then, but they had a great buzz and everyone was into their style.

During that tour, everybody got along great. There was a lot of partying on that tour, which helped me forget all the drama going on at home—relationship troubles. Metallica

had their own private jet, so they were able to fly from concert to concert. They would play until around midnight every night, shower up, and then take off for the airport. One night, I was hanging out with Kid Rock and he mentioned that he'd soon be going on *The Tonight Show* with Jay Leno. I came up with the bright idea to put a little wager on something. I told him that if he made a big cocaine reference right into the camera for me when he played his song, I'd give him a thousand bucks next time I saw him. It was a bet. If he didn't do it, he was gonna pay me a grand—and I really thought he wasn't gonna do it. With all the lights and cameras he'd be facing at *The Tonight Show* studio, I thought for sure he'd either get scared or forget all about it.

He didn't. I lost a thousand bucks.

Anyway, when we were talking about the proposed bet that night, Lars Ulrich, Metallica's drummer, came into the dressing room and jumped into conversation with us. He said Metallica was getting ready to take off in their private jet, and he invited me and Kid Rock to go with them.

Ride in Metallica's private jet?

Mmmm . . . let me think about that.

Before I could ponder, I had my bags in my hand, along with a little something I'd picked up after Korn's set: an eight-ball of cocaine. I felt like a fan who had won a contest; it was crazy. Sitting on that private plane with Kid Rock and Metallica was just surreal. I had a good time laughing and totally forgetting about the drama at home. But the laughter didn't last long. During the flight, I went into the bathroom and helped myself to my cocaine a couple times. That wiped the smile off my face as it always did; cocaine, despite its initial high, was always a good-time killer.

Three other guys (I'm not mentioning names) joined in with me on the cocaine after a while, and the stuff slowly took the fun out of their night, too. Well, one of them was having a pretty good time, but everybody else lost their smiles. Given that cocaine always had that effect, I never understood why we did it so much. I guess it was just the rock star thing to do; we all had to act our part.

The private jet ended up in Dallas, Texas, and we met up with the guys in the band Pantera at their night club. We kept snorting lines and lines of cocaine all night secretly in the club's back room. We didn't want anyone else around because we were all paranoid. We started talking in monotone voices, and our faces looked all white and scared, like deer in the headlights.

At around 4:00 A.M., something extremely weird happened. We were all locked up in the back room, wrapped up in a ridiculously serious but totally meaningless cocaine conversation about music. All of a sudden, one of the guys tried to throw in his two cents, but the cocaine had taken his ability to talk away; completely out of the blue, he'd become almost mute! It was so disturbing that I could barely keep myself together. Here I was, with this famous guy in a huger-than-life band, and his speech had almost completely stopped. He couldn't talk other than to slowly moan one word at a time. I got panicky because I'd given him the coke! No joke: news headlines flashed in my mind, "Head gives fellow rock star cocaine and causes him to lose ability to talk."

That night had started out like a surreal dream coming true, but it turned into a dark, gloomy dungeon. As I looked around the room at some of the top players in metal music, I started to think about where I was in life. I thought to myself, "Look at all of us. We're all on top of the music business, riding around in the best tour buses and flying in private jets. But here we are huddled in the back room of a night club hiding from everyone. Our faces are shining from cocaine sweat, we're talking nonsense, and one of us has lost the ability to speak a complete sentence!"

Although I didn't yet think of the problem in Christian terms, I see now that I had gained the whole world, but I was losing my soul. It was slipping away from me incredibly fast. Thankfully, that rock star was able to speak normally again the next day, but I couldn't stop thinking about what had happened. In fact, the question would haunt me for years: What was it benefiting me to "gain the whole world"?

I'd gained fame, but I'd lost the person that I was.

I'd gained money, but I'd lost my satisfaction and contentment in life.

I'd gained fans, but I was always away from the people that I loved the most.

Colossians 1:13-14 (THE MESSAGE)

God rescued us from dead-end alleys and dark dungeons. He's set us up in the kingdom of the Son he loves so much, the Son who got us out of the pit we were in, got rid of the sins we were doomed to keep repeating.

Despite the partial awakening I felt that night when I saw the damage that drugs could do, it took me a long time to act on it. Whether it was beer, cocaine, speed, or pills, I *still* kept on repeating the same stupid mistakes year after year— "doomed to keep repeating" them, as it says in Colossians. Every drug I mentioned above brought me complete misery after the short high wore off. After the thousands of beers I drank, mixed with the thousands of lines and pills I took, I could easily have died.

I could have lost my soul forever . . . but the Person who loved me the most rescued me before it was too late.

Now I am His forever. Who do *you* belong to?

DAY 2

Proverbs 3:5-6

Trust in the LORD with all your heart;
do not depend on your own understanding.
Seek his will in all you do, and he will
show you which path to take.

RECENTLY HAD TO FIGURE OUT how to trust the Lord with all my heart, while my heart was breaking.

I went with my friend Sonny, who sings for the band P.O.D., to visit a mutual friend of ours named Chi from the band Deftones. Chi had been in a horrible car accident ten months earlier, in November 2008; he was thrown from the vehicle because he wasn't wearing his seat belt. The accident left him in a coma for a while, but he'd improved somewhat and was now in a semiconscious state, so we wanted to pay him a visit.

Korn and Deftones started out together back in 1994 by playing in each other's hometowns. When we both finally got record deals, we hooked up a few times to tour together. Chi and I were a lot alike. We hung out because we loved our beer and we loved our girls back home. We didn't mess around with the hoochies on the road; we were the "good boys," at least in that regard. Chi just might be the nicest person I've

ever met on the planet. When I'd talk to him back in those touring days, it sometimes felt like he was a regular nice guy trapped in a rock star's body. But then when he'd hit the stage, the nice guy left and all you saw was a rockin' madman.

Even though I hadn't seen Chi in many years, I knew I had to do something to support him after I heard about his accident. I flew from Arizona and Sonny flew from southern California. We met up in northern California, where Chi was hospitalized, and rented a car for the last leg. My flight was very early in the morning, and I'd slept only about three hours the night before, so I was pretty tired when we landed. I don't drink coffee, but I pretty much woke up without caffeine when I saw the rental car that was given to me: a brand-new Camaro. That thing was sick! I hadn't even reserved it—not that car in particular—but there it was waiting for Sonny and me. At first, driving that car was fun, but knowing that we were going to visit Chi, who could have died in his car accident, brought me back to the hard reality I was going to face: my old friend was in critical condition, and it sucked bad.

When we arrived at Chi's mom's apartment, which was near the hospital, we received the warmest possible welcome. His mom, Jeanne, greeted us at the door while his sister, Mae, was cooking us breakfast. Their two dogs took a liking to us right away. They jumped all over us so much that Jeanne had to put them in a cage. The breakfast was awesome, and we just hung out for a while and talked before we went to the hospital, getting an update on Chi and catching up on news.

As we were getting ready to leave for the hospital, something cool happened. A couple weeks prior, Fieldy from Korn had organized a bunch of musicians to do a benefit song for Chi, and I asked Jeanne if she knew when Fieldy's song was gonna be released. She said she hadn't heard from him in a long time and didn't know. Then all of a sudden my phone rang. It was Fieldy, and he said he'd felt a strong urge to call me right then and didn't know why.

Very trippy.

Some people would call that crazy timing and some would call it divine timing, but *we* all knew it was the latter. Fieldy let me know that his song was going to be finished soon, and Jeanne was overwhelmed with excitement, sure that the momentum would help Chi. We all headed to the hospital with a strong sense that God was right there with us. Feeling God's presence helped relax the anxiety that had been building in me for days. I didn't know how to deal with such a catastrophe happening to someone that I'd known for so long.

When we arrived at the hospital and I saw Chi for the first time, my heart felt like it had shattered. I couldn't imagine what his family had been going through. I started praying for him immediately because I always try to go to God for everything as quick as I can. I prayed for a miracle, but just seeing the state he was in was incredibly hard, and believing that a miracle could happen was even harder.

As Jeanne and Mae talked to Chi and tried to get him to open his eyes, I started whispering cuss words to myself. I was so upset and emotional that instead of crying, I got mad. I couldn't understand how someone so nice and so loved could be going through something like that. Watching the still figure in the hospital bed, I saw a tattoo of Jesus on Chi's hand, and it made me think about how Jesus must've had a strong connection with Chi, because Jesus didn't deserve what happened to Him, either.

Jeanne and Mae stood back so that Sonny and I could talk to Chi, but all we could do was hope that he heard us. Chi was incoherent because of his semiconscious state and the many medicines he was on. Still, we kept talking to him, telling him that we loved him and that we wanted him to wake up and come back to his family.

We hung out there all day, breaking only for lunch with Jeanne and a visiting granddaughter, leaving Mae at Chi's side. During lunch, I realized where Chi had gotten his good nature, because Jeanne is such a sweetheart. We hung out at the restaurant for a while and then went back to the hospital to say goodbye to Chi. Man, I don't know if I'll ever hear a more heartfelt prayer than the one Sonny prayed for Chi before we left. We both just lay and cried on Chi's chest as Sonny softly prayed and begged God to bring our brother back.

God can make this happen, and I'm waiting to see it manifest. My heart was broken that day, and I've really had to trust in the Lord with my whole heart, as Proverbs 3:5–6 says in our scripture passage for the day. I'm trusting that God will turn the entire heartache that Chi's accident caused around for good in His way and with His timing.

As I write this, I don't know where Chi's recovery will be in the future, but I'm asking you, in the love of Jesus, to please go to the website OneLoveForChi.com and check his progress so you can know how to pray for him and his family. Chi's insurance canceled him because he wasn't showing signs of recovery fast enough for them. Please donate anything you can to help his family with the medical bills. Dealing with the aftermath of Chi's accident is horrible enough for his family, but the cancellation of his health insurance has been complete agony for them. Please help! Everybody can donate *something,* and the website makes it easy. Hopefully Chi will be out on tour with the Deftones by the time you read this.

Thank you very much, trust in the Lord with all your heart, and please wear your seat belt!

DAY 3

Genesis 6:6 (NIV)

The Lord was grieved that he had
made man on the earth, and his heart
was filled with pain.

HAVE YOU EVER HAD your heart broken so bad that you wished you weren't alive to feel the pain? The only relief from that sort of piercing heartbreak comes when you're sleeping. When you wake up in the morning, you wonder if the horrible experience was all a nightmare, but when reality sets in, the agonizing pain slowly pours into your heart as you awake. If we, as human beings, can feel that much pain after our hearts are shattered into a million pieces, then I wonder what it feels like for God to have His heart crushed as it says in Genesis 6:6, above. First John 4 tells us that God is love. God is where love comes from and he is what love is all about. I can't even imagine what it would feel like for pure love to be "filled with pain."

A lot of us humans, if we believe in God at all, tend to think that God is this big ol' strict, grandpa-like judge in the sky who's ready to slam the hammer down when anybody does anything wrong.

That's not true at all, as the Bible tells us.

We are all made in God's image. The emotions that we feel, God felt first. Psalm 50:2 says God is the perfection of beauty, and He shines in glorious radiance. Jeremiah 31:3 says God has loved us with an everlasting love and has drawn us to Himself with loving-kindness. Beauty, loving-kindness—that's the complete opposite of a strict, grandpa-like judge in the sky.

He made all of humanity from the depths of His heart of perfect spiritual beauty and loving-kindness. He's the master artist. God looks at us humans with love because that's His nature. When the human race rebelled against God, it pierced the very existence of Divine Love Himself. Like the purest, clearest glass being shattered by a ball, God's heart was shattered by the people He created, who were made in the image of love. It's just crazy to think that God's heart was "filled with pain" over the human race He created. He could've said, "Forget everything. I'm gonna wipe them all out forever!"

But God had a higher plan than that. He didn't want to go and make a bunch of robots He could control. He wanted us to *choose* Him. God set out a plan to teach the broken human race about the love and relationship that He created for all of us to have with Himself. That's exactly where things went wrong, and that's exactly where we have to get back to. The most important lesson that we're supposed to be learning right now is how completely lost we are without God. If we don't learn this lesson, then our lives are going to have zero meaning. If that's how we end up—still disconnected from God—then we might as well say this: "We came here by chance and we're withering away into nothing."

There's zero purpose in that. It makes no sense.

Exodus 34:6-7

The Lord passed in front of Moses, calling out, "Yahweh! The Lord! The God of compassion and mercy! I am slow to anger and filled with unfailing love and faithfulness. I lavish unfailing love to a thousand generations. I forgive iniquity, rebellion, and sin. But I do not excuse the guilty."

We are all born into rebellion. It's not our fault, but it's the truth. We are all corrupt and in need of forgiveness, unfailing love, compassion, and mercy. That's how it is, even if we sit here all day and try to make our case: "I didn't ask to be born, so how am I guilty?" or "I'm a good person! I've never robbed a bank or even stolen a library book."

The fact is, we didn't ask to be here, but we all *are* here. We were all born into corruption, and we all have to die because of one man's disobedience (Romans 5:15). It doesn't matter how good we've been in our lives; we're all imperfect and we're all going to die one day.

We all need to just stop, shut up about how good we are (or aren't), and say, "You are God, and You have set things in motion the way You, perfect Divine Love, wanted things to work. I will choose to learn about love from You because You *are* love. I want to trust You. I was born and I'm going to die and I have none of the answers. Please teach me by allowing me to experience your divine love. Teach me about receiving Your love and giving You love through Jesus, so I can learn what life and love are really all about."

Amen.

DAY 4

1 Samuel 17:47

[Preparing to meet Goliath, David said,]
"And everyone assembled here will know that
the Lord rescues his people, but not with
sword and spear. This is the Lord's battle,
and he will give you to us!"

'VE NEVER BEEN much of a fighter. In fact, I was a total wimp as a kid, something I discovered when I was in the sixth grade. My class had a mix of fifth- and sixth-grade kids. At the beginning of the sixth-grade school year, I noticed that the fifth graders looked up to us sixth graders, so we generally got to have our way when disagreements happened. I kind of liked that, so I would act like the older brother type to the fifth graders, bossing them around a little. I was never a bully, but I did try to exploit their fear a bit after I found out they were just naturally intimidated by me.

One day I went too far and this little blond fifth grader, a kid named Johnny, told me we were gonna fight after school to sort out what we'd been arguing about. But Johnny wasn't a normal little blond-haired kid; he lived in the gang neighborhoods and talked like the Hispanic kids, even though he was white. Johnny said something like, "After school, *esé*, I'm gonna beat you up!" I was shocked. This little fifth grader wanted to *fight* me! I started getting scared when I noticed that he and the other Hispanic kids were whispering and staring at me with grins on their faces. Were they gonna jump me? I didn't know, but I wasn't going to find out.

I told the fifth grader that I didn't want to fight him. I felt like a wimp, but I went home having learned a lesson: don't try to be tough unless you want to back it up. After that episode I tried not to get tough with anyone again. I got picked on over the years, but I never got myself into anything like I did with little *esé* Johnny!

But just because I'd resolved not to start fights didn't mean that fights didn't sometimes have a way of finding me. When I was sixteen, I went to a small party at a local apartment where I met up with my friends Terry and Kelly. There were a bunch of people I didn't know there, and a few minutes after I arrived I noticed one guy staring at me. He looked really mad, so I tried to avert my eyes and mind my own business. The next thing I knew, the right side of my face was numb. I didn't really feel the impact itself, but this guy had punched me in the face for no reason . . . or so I thought.

I had a friend named Richard who lived on the other side of town, and most people thought that he and I looked a lot alike. We both had "pig noses." After the punch hit, I realized that the guy was calling me Richard and saying I'd messed around with his girlfriend. My friends rushed over and held him back as I tried to convince him that I wasn't Richard. The next thing I knew, Kelly and Terry had taken the guy outside. When they returned about five minutes later, they looked a bit tense. I asked them what was wrong, and they said that they'd taken care of the guy who'd hit me. I was the type of guy who never made trouble, so my friends had felt bad about the surprise attack and had kicked that guy's booty. Whoa! I wasn't even famous yet and I had bodyguards!

So basically I was never much of a fighter, and that's pretty much how it was when I got famous with Korn. We never had to fight our own battles. We hired big, tough friends to take care of everything. I asked one of our bodyguards on the first day he worked for us what kind of fight training he knew.

"I know crazy, Homes," he said.

Okay, if crazy will do the job, then you're hired!

These bodyguards would do anything we asked them to do. I never had them hit anyone, but a couple of the other Korn members got into some drama once or twice. In the beginning, when Korn first started touring—this was before we had bodyguards—we went on tour with Marilyn Manson. We were pretty good friends with everyone on the tour at that time. One night when everyone was all drunk, Manson's bus driver and some other dudes got into it with Korn's bass player, Fieldy. They messed with him pretty hard and held him down until he couldn't breathe. It got serious, but they let him go eventually. Fieldy didn't do anything because they probably would've jumped him if he'd tried.

Now fast-forward five years to when Korn had made it big and we had our big ol' bodyguards. One night, when we were all out on the town in some city that I don't remember, Fieldy spotted Manson's bus driver as we were walking the streets. As soon as he noticed him, he yelled to our security guard, "See that guy right there? Go get him and rip his face off!" The guy took off running down the street—and lucky for him, our bodyguard didn't catch him.

Looking back on it now, I see all that kind of behavior in a new way. Having protection, having bodyguards—that's kind of how things get handled with God when we have horrible circumstances in our lives. I don't have bodyguards anymore; instead, I have God. He's the ultimate bodyguard—stronger than any other force out there. He doesn't kick and punch or seek revenge idly. He doesn't dole human-style justice out whenever I feel like I've been wronged. But he always has my back, no matter what kind of fight I may be up against in life.

In our daily verse, the young King David knew that going up against the massive Philistine fighter Goliath could end terribly for him. Goliath was a giant and David was really just a kid still, the youngest of all his brothers. But he trusted that God would fight the battle for him. This is something that we all need to learn. We have to let go and let God be our defender. If the circumstances are out of our control, *we* can't make anything happen. All we can do is tell God our situation and ask him to fight for us. We don't tell him to make someone else's life miserable if that person has made us mad. No, our job is to bless and pray for that person and let God deal with him. Joyce Meyer, a respected Bible teacher, says that "hurting people" are the ones who hurt other people. If we keep that in mind when people hurt us, it can help take the sting out of whatever pain may have come to us.

So whatever you're going through right now, give it to the Lord to fight for you. Maybe you're not going through anything right now, but we both know you will be one day. When it does happen, the best thing you can do is:

Give the battle to the Lord.

After you let go and place your burdens in God's hands, try to rest in the fact that God will eventually take care of things for you. Find your peace and then stay there, because He will never reject anyone who humbles him- or herself and asks for God's helping hand.

DAY 5

Hebrews 12:10-11 (NIV)

Our fathers disciplined us for a
little while as they thought best; but God
disciplines us for our good, that we may
share in his holiness. No discipline seems
pleasant at the time, but painful. Later
on, however, it produces a harvest
of righteousness and peace for those
who have been trained by it.

TATTOOS HURT.

If anyone tells you that repeatedly sticking a needle
into your body to get a tattoo doesn't hurt, they're lying
through their teeth. I've got tattoos on my arms, hands, back,
face, neck, stomach, chest, leg, and palm, and every single one
of them hurt. I'm getting one in my armpit next. It's gonna
say, "He lifted me out of the slimy pit" (Psalm 40:2, NIV).

Clever, right? Ha-ha! I'm a nut job and I love it! And Jesus
is crazy about me. He's crazy about all of us; He can't help
it. And just as Jesus shows his love for us in different ways,
every Christian chooses to express his or her love for God in a

unique manner. As you might have guessed, tattoos are a big part of my expression.

I guess the main reason I like to express myself by getting tattoos is the line of work I'm in. I don't have to work a normal job, so that gives me a lot of freedom. Most metal musicians are the same way, often inked top to bottom. Nowadays, it seems like the people who don't have tattoos in the metal music world are the oddballs. It's just how it is.

I had only a few tattoos before I became a Christian, but the ones I did get were very meaningful to me. The word "issues" on my right forearm was tattooed on me when I was going through my divorce. Another one from that time period—an art piece on my right arm—symbolized me starting over in life. The two names on the back of my neck are of my daughter Jennea and a daughter I gave up for adoption (who's someone else's beloved daughter now). I guess a lot of my tattoos are memorials of pain, reminding me that I've gotten through a lot of heartache in my life so far. The Christian tattoos are reminders to me that God brought me through the worst of my pain and that he will be there with me to face all the pain I have in the future as well. The second half of life is where most people face the most pain, so I'm glad I have all these beautiful art pieces reminding me that I can get through anything with the strength Jesus gives me.

I've been through a lot for the tattoos on my body, and I have enough ink on me to know that getting that armpit tattoo is gonna hurt. Under the arms has got to be one of the most sensitive areas on the body—ouch! Though I must say, getting a tattoo on my palm was an interesting experience of pain. Grab something sharp or use your fingernail to scratch your palm. It feels kinda weird, right? The nerves make it so that it both hurts and tickles.

When I got my palm tattoo, I was in Canada visiting my friend Todd. He took me to the shop where he got all his ink done, and originally I'd planned on getting only one tattoo near my neck. The artist told me about a Mafia member that he'd once tattooed on the hand, and apparently that tattoo had made the "tough guy" scream like a girl. I told him I was thinking about getting a tattoo on my hand that said, "DT 28:13"—standing for Deuteronomy 28:13, which says, "The Lord will make you the *head* and not the tail" (italics added). He said he could do it, but even with all my experience with ink, I was kind of afraid after hearing how the Mafia guy had carried on.

At the end of the day, though, I did it. It took about three guys to hold my hand and arm still as I got that tattoo. Each time the needle went into my skin, I felt the weirdest sensation. It hurt like hell and tickled at the same time, and though I tried not to scream at all, out of my mouth came the strangest noise I think I've ever made—a combination of a scream and a laugh. In the end, though, the tattoo came out just as I'd envisioned it.

A few months later, I came up with another one of my "brilliant" ideas. I made a trip to L.A. and decided to go to three different tattoo artists to get as much work done as I could. Two brothers named Mikey and Tommy Montoya totally sleeved my left arm the first couple days in L.A. Mikey did the Korn CD cover for *Untouchables* on my lower-left forearm, and Tommy did a portrait of Jennea beneath a picture of the famous statue of Jesus in Rio de Janeiro, Brazil, on my upper arm. The following day another dude in Hollywood did my record company's logo, "H2C," as a back piece. I had it done in red, and it looks like blood is dripping down my back.

I didn't know it ahead of time, but all the pain endorphins in my body were completely shot by the beginning of that third day. I lay down on the guy's tattoo bench and he stuck the stencil on my back. Then he went over it with a regular ink pen to fill in the faded lines. I should have suspected right then that my pain endorphins were shot, because even that ballpoint pen hurt! When he actually started the tattoo, it felt like he was literally carving chunks of flesh out of me with a knife. I practically jumped out of my skin. I simply couldn't lie still. I think I even shed a tear. The artist couldn't do any straight lines because I was moving so much. All we could finish that day was the outline of the piece.

My friend Walter Frank, who worked at Chester Bennington's Club Tattoo in Phoenix, ended up finishing the "H2C" back piece for me later on. I was so traumatized by the first experience that I had to have him use a powerful numbing ointment on my back—something that had been invented for severe burn victims.

An artist named Killer tattooed the name Jesus on my palm in 2005 after I got saved. At the same time he tattooed some flames on the back of my hand. I don't know if this dude's hands were heavy or what, but man, I could barely stand getting that tattoo. The pain was up there with the back piece, though nothing can really compare to *that* pain. I remember my hand throbbing in agony as Killer was finishing the tattoo. I actually threw in the towel before it was done because I couldn't take anymore . . . until a friend of mine, Bill Vanboeing, who had tattooed the "issues" piece and the art piece symbolizing me starting over on my forearm, came in the shop and called me a punk. I thought I'd show him, so I decided to man up and get the tattoo. The result? An hour after the tattoo was finished my hand had swelled up to double its usual size. No joke! In fact, I was planning to go to the hospital the next day if it didn't go back to normal. Yeah, it was that bad. Luckily, by the morning the swelling had gone down quite a bit. But man, was it sore for days afterward.

Obviously, the pain isn't my favorite part of getting tattoos, but it's a part of the process I have to go through in order to get the cool art on my skin that makes me proud when I see it. It's a totally different way of looking at words and images from the Bible. A totally different way of projecting my faith. While the pain is hard, it's worth it because the finished product adds a new layer onto my faith and offers a visual representation of my experience that I can share with others.

I'm an artist because I *love* art. The art of music, the art of pictures, paintings—*any* type of art is awesome to me. It totally speaks its own language of the heart. But with art creations, there's usually a long process before you get to see the finished product. In the same way, each of us is one of God's art pieces. He has to shape us and mold us like clay in order to turn us into the works of art that He desires. Oftentimes, it's a painful discipline we have to endure, but in the end, we are God's masterpieces. And just like most artistic creations, there's a long process that God takes us through in order to make our character shine like Christ's.

By getting tattoos, I feel that I'm doing my part as one of God's masterpieces by becoming a literal work of His art. By doing so, I share His holiness with everyone I connect with. Holiness isn't some obnoxious religious word. Holiness is the very character of God—perfection, beauty, love, majesty, power, pure goodness. God wants to share His character and nature with us, but there's a price we have to pay on our part. We have to trust God with everything we have inside of us, because, as today's scripture passage from Hebrews reminds us, "no discipline seems pleasant at the time, but painful. Later on, however, it produces a harvest of righteousness and peace for those who have been trained by it."

DAY 6

Psalm 91:1 (NKJV)

He who dwells in the secret place
of the Most High

Shall abide under the shadow
of the Almighty.

'VE BEEN IN A RELATIONSHIP with Jesus for over five years now, and one of the most important things I've learned is how to dwell—or, as the dictionary puts it, to be a "permanent resident"—in the secret place of the Most High.

There are a lot of reasons why God is called the Most High. Perhaps most obviously, that label means He is the highest authority over all creation because everything comes from Him, but I'd like to bring up another interpretation. When I envision God as the Most High, I'm reminded of how God has made me feel higher than any drug I've ever taken. So many times God has completely intoxicated me with His love. It's not me being emotional or weird, either. Those experiences are actually God pouring His love into me, responding to my desire to be in a real relationship with Him. To be in a healthy relationship with another person, you have to experience that person by giving and receiving love; otherwise, it's not a real relationship at all. It's the same thing in a relationship with God. This isn't some fake religion I'm after. I'm after a real relationship with the One who loved me and gave Himself to save me from myself.

The Holy Spirit is poured out like wine on those who give up the desires of the world and crave a real relationship with God. Matthew 9:17 says that when we believe in Jesus, the Spirit of God is poured into us like new wine into new wineskins (the containers they carried their drinks in back in the day). This "wine," as the Holy Spirit is figuratively called, is better than any drug—or anything else in creation, for that matter. It's the highest high any person can ever experience on this earth. Unfortunately, it's hard for people to actually let go of themselves and the world enough to experience God in this way. Worse yet, many people don't believe that they *can* experience God so intimately.

What I feel that God is trying to say to us with Psalm 91:1 in our daily passage is this: all people who learn to live as permanent residents in the secret place of their mind (thoughts) and heart (feelings) with God will be protected and intoxicated with God's love, remaining stable in a state of rest under the "shadow of the Almighty." The Bible clearly states that Christ is in us and we are seated with Him in heavenly realms. We have to tap into this reality by experiencing God's breathtaking gift inside of us. Believe me, once this becomes real to you, no bad news that comes into your life will be able to move you from this strong foundation inside of you.

Many of the difficult experiences I've had as a Christian came with a major choice I was forced to make. In those experiences, my confusion would sometimes be so great that I wouldn't know what direction to take. Those were the best times for me to "live as a permanent resident in the secret place" of my heart, trusting God no matter what things looked like around me. I've always pictured the "shadow of the Almighty" as a gigantic tree protecting me from the thunderous storm clouds. In my times of need, I feel I'm under that huge tree, waiting for my mental and emotional storms to pass; and when they pass, the sun shines again, giving me clarity to make the decisions that I need to make.

We can *all* learn to walk in such a close relationship with God—so close that no difficulty or tragedy will be able to move us from our trust in Him: trust that He'll turn everything around for good for those who love Him (Romans 8:28). It doesn't matter what we're experiencing: broken relationships, loss of a house or car, illness or a death in the family. Anything that comes our way will be like thunderous storm clouds opening up to hurl their rain and hailstones down—not on us, but on the gigantic tree that hovers over us in protection.

If you don't feel this strong in your relationship with God right now, I urge you to invest daily personal time with Him. I'm no expert, but that kind of daily relational work has helped me look at life's difficulties as exercise equipment intended to build up my spiritual muscles of faith in the One who watches over us all. Draw near to God and God will draw near to you, the Bible tells us (James 4:8). Don't worry: life's troubles can be viewed as a school of God's Spirit teaching you awesome things that you never knew. Relax, be at peace, and learn.

DAY 7

Galatians 6:8 (ESV)

For the one who sows to his own flesh
will from the flesh reap corruption,
but the one who sows to the Spirit will
from the Spirit reap eternal life.

ENTER MY CHILDHOOD YEARS...
My motto used to be: If a little bit of something
makes me feel good, then a lot of it will make me feel
way better! Before I became a teenager, junk food ruled my
life. I got a lot of vitamin C and vitamin S in my diet: cheese
and sugar. As might have been expected, I struggled with
weight as a kid because of the way I ate. When I started getting made fun of for being fat, I went on a diet and curbed the
junk food to try to get skinny like my friends. I thought that
if I could get rid of my fat belly, my friends wouldn't pick on
me so much. But after I hit puberty, I got tall and skinny and
didn't have to worry about *that* anymore.

Enter my teenage years...
When I was a sophomore in high school, my friend Reggie
and I hung out a lot, and we started getting drunk together.
My motto still held firm: If a little bit of something makes me

feel good, then a lot of it will make me feel way better. Now, though, I had a perpetual mess waiting to happen. That was around the time I got introduced to Mr. Toilet, Mr. Puke, and Mr. Hangover, but that didn't dissuade me from my motto.

Not too long after we started drinking, Reggie and I found ourselves partying at least three days a week. We played "Hey, Mister" at the liquor stores (that's when you ask a grown-up outside a store to buy you alcohol when you're underage) and broke into my dad's bar at home, drinking his stash. We went to keg parties, drank harder stuff at band practice—I'd started making music by then—and basically chugged whatever we could get our hands on to get our buzz. I'd been able to get a handle on the food thing when I was younger, but this alcohol thing was totally different.

Just as our daily Bible verse from Galatians says, I was sowing to my flesh what felt good, and then paying the price for it the morning after. Yet no matter how bad I felt, I just couldn't stop drinking—probably because I didn't really want to. Life wasn't acceptable when sobriety ruled because I didn't like "me." I was so insecure that in order to feel good about myself, I needed a mask to hide behind and a can of beer for courage.

Enter the Korn years . . .

Part of the deal when you play a concert is that the promoter has to supply food and beverages to the band. Every day of every show, we had a dressing room that looked like a Coors Light commercial. Cases of beer cans on ice seemed to yell, "Drink me! Drink me!" I couldn't resist. Once again, I sowed into my flesh and reaped physical destruction: drunk at night with a hangover during the day.

As the years passed, I noticed that though I continued to drink, the fun slipped away more and more, while the depression became stronger and stronger. The beer wasn't doing the trick anymore, so I started messing with coke and speed until . . . you know the story: I found myself flat on my face in a scummy gutter with a huge, junky addiction to methamphetamines.

My childhood motto had become my prison.

Last, but certainly not least, enter Jesus . . .

When Jesus first entered my life, He slowly taught me how to lay my flesh and all the evil I sowed to it into a grave. It was surprisingly easy for me to do then, because when I felt His presence, I was completely satisfied and I didn't *want* to hang on to my old ways of living anymore. After I'd given up my old life, Jesus showed me how to start a new life, sowing to please His Spirit. He's also been showing me that the reaping of eternal life that our daily scripture mentions doesn't happen only when I die. It happens *now,* as my soul connects with eternity after sowing to please the eternal Spirit. It started the day I gave Jesus my life, and it will continue to grow now and forever.

There's no doubt that most people reading my words have at least some experience sowing to the flesh. But if we keep going back to the things that bring negativity into our lives, we're never going to change. Proverbs 26:11 gives proof of what I'm trying to say:

As a dog returns to its vomit,
so a fool repeats his foolishness.

So, what do you say? Let's agree to stop sowing to our flesh and let's stay away from the vomit.

DAY 8

Romans 7:15-18

I don't really understand myself,
for I want to do what is right, but
I don't do it. Instead, I do what I hate.
But if I know that what I am doing is wrong,
this shows that I agree that the law
is good. So I am not the one doing
wrong; it is sin living in me that does
it. And I know that nothing good
lives in me, that is, in my sinful nature.
I want to do what is right, but I can't.

WHEN I FINALLY DECIDED to turn my life around, one of the best decisions I ever made was to quit my career and stay at home to take care of Jennea. I had been living as someone else up until that point in my life, so now I wanted my daughter to get to know the real me. Actually, *I* wanted to get to know the real me, too. To accomplish my goal, I set my heart on becoming a good dad.

Little did I know, I had a hard battle ahead of me.

The first time I realized that the old me wouldn't disappear overnight came when I was getting ready for a missionary trip to India. The passport agency and I battled back and forth as I tried to get a replacement for a passport I'd misplaced. While driving to the passport office with five-year-old Jennea in the backseat, I got my directions confused. All I seemed able to do was drive in circles, hopelessly lost. I'd been arguing with the agency for days, and now getting lost was the last straw.

When my frustration reached its boiling point, I went insane. I started beating the steering wheel and windshield while slamming on the brakes at the same time. The car skidded off to the side of the road as I screamed and growled, more like an animal than a human being. Once stopped, I jumped out of the car, kicking it and screaming like a maniac, "*Why,* God?! *Why,* God?! #%&!"

Jennea, of course, remained buckled in the backseat. She screamed and sobbed in shock. And why shouldn't she? Her own father had skidded his car off the road, let more expletives than necessary fly from his mouth, and repeatedly and viciously kicked his BMW 750!

When I finally composed myself, I went to the car and did my best to calm Jennea down. Then I drove off again, determined to find my destination. I did . . . eventually.

After I parked the car, I turned back to Jennea. Smiling reassuringly, I said, "Stay inside the car until I get back. I have some business to take care of, but I won't be long." Then I locked the doors and left. When I got back to the car, I found that Jennea had rolled down her window and was crying her heart out to some lady.

So much for my goal of being a great dad. Man, I felt more like an abusive father—especially with the way that lady looked at me. I decided to do a little damage control. "Everything is fine," I told the lady. Then I thanked her for being a concerned citizen and shooed her away.

And yet, my sweet daughter had been traumatized . . . by me—her dad.

I'm glad to say circumstances aren't that dramatic anymore, but I still do things I wish I could take back. As the saying goes, "You always hurt the ones you love the most." Nowadays, Jennea sometimes annoys me for acting like an obnoxious preteen, so I (acting like a preteen myself) overreact in anger and do things that I hate myself for later, like thumping her on the head with my finger, or yanking her ponytail for lying to me— not exactly the best parenting skills. But those things haven't happened in a while, so I am slowly but surely improving. I would have to say the most irritating thing I do to her—acting more like an annoying big brother than a dad—is constantly pick on her and joke with her. I can't seem to shake my warped, annoying big-brother personality. That's not the person I want to be to my daughter, but my personality has been molded over the years, and old habits unfortunately die hard.

I once met a woman who commented that Jennea and I were pretty much growing up together. That bums me out because I know it's true: I suppressed my emotions by getting drunk and high for so many years that I didn't mature in the usual progression. I live that reality. My worst fear is that I'll finally reach the maturity Jennea deserves when it's too late and Jennea's all grown up. But I can't lose hope, and I'm not gonna give up trying to change. I'll keep on trying and praying like crazy. I make a point to pray with Jennea and ask her and God for forgiveness every time I screw up (which happens a lot), and I try to lean on the *Lord's* perfection to make up for my severe lack of it. I love Jennea with all my heart and I'm so proud of her. She's such a great kid, man. As I write these confessions, I'm feeling pretty emotional, so I'd like to write a personal note to Jennea:

*I couldn't have been blessed with a more amazing daughter
than you, Jennea. I know I don't show it all the time, but
I love you more than words can express, and I couldn't be
more proud of you. You are growing into a beautiful young
woman, sweet and kind-hearted. Even when your preteen
attitude kicks in, you're easy to deal with. Nea, please forgive
me for every pain I've caused you. I sincerely regret all of my
angry reactions. One of my biggest prayers for you is that
God will bring you a way better man than your dad when
you're all grown up. I haven't represented how a man should
treat you the way you deserve. You should be treated like a
princess, the way Jesus treats His bride, the church.*

> *Thank you for being such
> a great daughter!*
>
> *Love,
> Dad*

Some people say I'm too hard on myself, but I think it's
good to want to be the best dad I can be. It's good to feel
sorrow for the mistakes I've made in life. It's good to lean on
the Lord for all things.

I can totally relate to what Paul is talking about in our daily
passage from Romans 7. Like Paul, I don't really understand
myself either. I want to be a great dad to Jennea, but sometimes I just can't do it. Instead, I often do what I hate and
overreact in anger.

I know that everyone reading this book can relate with the
daily scripture. We all do things we hate, because we're imperfect people. All I can say is, I'm with you in this struggle.
We just need to always try our best, ask God to change us, and
ask everybody we've hurt for forgiveness. We should never

try to sweep the messes we make under the rug. We always have to address our difficult situations, pour out our hearts to encourage communication, and let the healing begin.

Let's make a deal together: I'll never give up if you don't.

Agreed?

DAY 9

2 Corinthians 5:5 (NIV)

Now it is God who has made us for this very purpose and has given us the Spirit as a deposit, guaranteeing what is to come.

DEPOSIT

- To give as security or in part payment
- A sum payable as a first installment on the purchase of something or as a pledge for a contract, the balance being payable later

GUARANTEE

- Something that gives a certainty of outcome
- A formal promise or assurance that certain conditions will be fulfilled

In the Bible, Jesus refers to an "Advocate" that will come after his ascension to those who believe. This "Advocate" is the Holy Spirit. Jesus also calls the Holy Spirit "he," not "it." This tells us that the Spirit is a divine being—real and separate from Jesus and separate from the Father, but also one with them. Kind of like the sun, the sun's heat, and the sun's light. Each is a part of the sun, but each also has its own thing going on.

Similar to how a bank receives money for a down payment for a house, we have received down payment of our eternal life from God via the gift of the Holy Spirit. This is what today's scripture from 2 Corinthians is all about. We (the bank) can actually hold our deposit (the Holy Spirit) in our hands and experience its value every day if we want. Or we can choose to put it away and forget about it, going on with business as usual.

Our deposit/gift from God also comes with a guarantee: the peace and 100 percent certainty of what's to come. The Bible says that no eye has seen, no ear has heard, and no mind has conceived all that God has prepared for those who love Him. But God has given us a peek, a glimpse of what awaits us (1 Cor 2:9–10). We can taste heaven if we choose to make use of our deposit (the Holy Spirit) and experience God.

Check out these words that Jesus spoke:

John 14:16–17

And I will ask the Father, and he will give you another Advocate, who will never leave you. He is the Holy Spirit, who leads into all truth. The world cannot receive him, because it isn't looking for him and doesn't recognize him. But you know him, because he lives with you now and later will be in you.

John 14:20

When I am raised to life again, you
will know that I am in my Father, and
you are in me, and I am in you.

Ephesians 2:6

For he raised us from the dead along
with Christ and seated us with him
in the heavenly realms because we
are united with Christ Jesus.

The most awesome thing that the Holy Spirit does is enable himself, Jesus, and God our Father—together known as the Trinity—to live with us and inside of us as we walk the earth (John 14:20). The Spirit also enables us to live with the Trinity in heaven in the hidden person of our heart at the same time (Ephesians 2:6). Now, I know that when you first read these things you'll want to scratch your head and ask, "Huh? How?" We can't fully understand all God's ways, no matter how many times we read a passage. It's a mystery, accepted by faith at first; but the supernatural is a reality that *all people* can actually experience if they humble themselves and believe like a child.

Childlike belief is simple. It doesn't doubt, but trusts—no matter the circumstances. For those of you who are around little kids, you know what I mean. They'll believe whatever you say or do because it's *you;* they'll trust whatever comes out of your mouth. The Bible is sometimes called the word of God. It came out of God's mouth, so we should believe His word above all else—even if some of it is hard to believe or understand at first. If we make the choice to believe and ask the Spirit to help us understand, everything will start to become real to us as the Holy Spirit rewards us for believing God's word before we experience it.

Let me try to explain more. Do you feel emotions inside when someone you love pours affection on you? Like a girl-friend, boyfriend, husband, wife, friend, child, or parent? You sense that, right? And it's a nice feeling, so we find ourselves opening our heart to those people easily. The same is true with the Lord. Our Advocate, the Holy Spirit, will train us in intimacy with God the Father and Jesus the Son. Soon we will feel the affection from heaven poured into our hearts more and more. And it's more real than any human affection we could experience, because God *created* human emotions. He knows just what we need to feel loved.

As a musician, I've made millions of dollars on the stage. I used to joke that I had won the lottery. You see, playing music isn't *work* to me—I'd do it for free because being able to create music is a gift in itself. When God filled me with His Spirit after I gave my life to Jesus, I knew I was being given another gift—the most expensive gift that has ever been given. I felt like I'd won the ultimate lottery of the universe. I didn't have to do anything to get this gift; it was given to me simply because *I wanted God.* And that free gift made me want to give God everything in my life.

Out of all the choices you have in your life, I beg you to make the choice to dive into the deep oceans of the Bible. If you do, the Holy Spirit will help you find what you're looking for.

Jeremiah 29:13 (NASB)

You will seek Me and find Me when you
search for Me with all your heart.

DAY 10

GROWING UP IN THE '80S, I had a favorite fast-food restaurant (with big golden arches) where my parents
used to take me. This place had prizes for kids and play
areas I liked to climb on. The burgers and fries were good
and greasy—just the way I liked them. In fact, I liked the restaurant so much that I've been eating there off and on pretty
much my whole life. But toward the end of my time in Korn,
I started going to that restaurant for a completely different
reason: straws.

I was so drawn to the straws. They weren't like the straws
at other fast-food restaurants. Nope, these straws were a lot
wider, and you could slurp a lot more soda from them . . . or
shakes . . . or crystal methamphetamine. What? Yep, I used to

make special trips to the golden arches just to get the big fat straws so that I could snort big fat lines at my big fat house or in my big fat tour bus.

It's weird to see something that I associate so strongly with my childhood overlaid with another, much more sinister meaning. How did I sink so low? Was it my rock star lifestyle? Was it because my wife left and took half of my money? Was it because I needed something to keep me high after playing in front of gigantic crowds? Why was my sober life not enough? Why were those straws so incredibly important?

I don't know the answers to any of those questions for sure. What I do know is that after snorting lines every day with my big fat straws for two years, I needed someone to help me or I was gonna die.

I tried quitting on my own.

Didn't work.

I tried going to rehab.

Didn't work.

Then, as a last resort, I tried going to church with a friend.

Didn't work. Well, on second thought, I was able to quit for a week or two, and I got some great advice from the pastor there, but I was still powerless to resist that dirty drug until one day when I had the best thing happen to me that ever happened in my life.

Before that day, I'd thought Jesus was just a story about a guy in history that nobody could prove true or false. I assumed that people who believed in Jesus weren't very secure in who they were.

Then all of a sudden Jesus Himself, not a preacher or any purely human man, came to me through the Holy Spirit and showed me, revealing to my heart and mind, that He was God—whether I believed or not. That incredible experience

I had with God changed my heart in a moment. Not completely and totally, but a radical change definitely took place in me that keeps growing and expanding even to this day. In a matter of seconds, I went from thinking people who believed in Jesus were stupid to knowing the truth.

All at once, Jesus revealed himself to me, just as His own word says he will do in John 14:21. Jesus can do the same thing for any of you who are reading this, if you're hungry for a relationship with Him and you're willing to change your life in whichever way He leads. Maybe some of you have seen Christians as weak and weird, like I used to, but now you're thinking, "Hey, maybe I've been wrong this whole time." If God can change a spiritually blind person like me and convince me to admit that I was wrong about Jesus, He can and will do it for you if you desire.

The way it happens isn't the same for everyone. The circumstances for you will be your own; they will be on your own clock, in your own location, and for your own purpose. But when He does find you, it's always for the same reason: to start a relationship with you that will always grow and last forever. To keep you from death. To bring you into His love—forever. You can't escape His love. He will never stop loving you and chasing you down so you can belong only to Him. Start searching for Jesus and learning about Him now, and if you don't give up, He will eventually reveal himself to you.

DAY 11

Mark 5:2, 5 (AMP), 15 (NLT)

And as soon as He got out of the boat, there met Him out of the tombs a man [under the power] of an unclean spirit. . . . Night and day among the tombs and on the mountains he was always shrieking and screaming and beating and bruising and cutting himself with stones. . . . A crowd soon gathered around Jesus, and they saw the man who had been possessed by the legion of demons. He was sitting there fully clothed and perfectly sane, and they were all afraid.

RECENTLY I PUT MY HOUSE on the market, and most of the people who came by to see it participated in a survey about their overall opinion of the place. Almost every comment was the same: the house was priced well and in a good area, but the holes in the walls, especially in the master bedroom, made a bad impression. The potential buyers must've thought I'd had huge parties at my house, but there wasn't a single party thrown in that house during the three years I lived there. Instead, the holes came from a dark and scary season in my life.

I remember many years ago hearing about a self-injurious teen trend called "cutting" that was on the rise. It's something that some teens were/are doing to physically hurt themselves when their emotions are either too numb or too intense to deal with. When I was a kid, I'd never heard of people injuring themselves on purpose, so it sounded crazy to me when I first heard about the cutting trend as an adult. Now, though, I think I can relate a little more to these kids who injure themselves, because in 2006 I dealt with a lot of out-of-control emotions and behaviors that were . . . well, horrifying.

I've mentioned before that at the beginning of my Christian life I felt bliss and peace, but there came a time in my walk with God that He had to allow difficult circumstances and dark storms to enter, in order to bring all my inner demons to the surface. I'm telling you right now, when those storms came, I turned into another person. Depression, darkness, gloom, anger, rage, and insanity would consume me about every other week for months. I'd feel great one week and be a total basket case the next. At one point I thought I was completely losing my mind!

Whenever the rage hit me, I would run into my bedroom and start punching my walls and screaming at the top of my lungs. If my daughter was at home, I had to go into the walk-in closet in my bedroom and wig out there so that Jennea wouldn't hear "Dad losing his mind" again. Let me just say, a lot of twisted stuff went on in that closet. Like a freakin' monster, I would get on my knees and scream at the top of my lungs. When it got really bad, I beat myself on the face and head. The worst of it came when I'd get a metal belt and whip myself on the back until I had welts on my skin. After a few of these episodes, I started to understand what those kids who cut themselves were going through. I felt like the man in today's scriptural passage—the one who was "shrieking and screaming and beating and bruising and cutting himself," though minus the cutting.

These episodes of madness would last about ten or fifteen minutes and then go away. After that, I would just get up, blow the snot out of my nose from all the screaming and wailing, and lie around for a couple days. I'm sure that if people had a spiritual glimpse of me in the closet back in those days, most would have seen an "unclean spirit" in me. Hurting myself might not have been the smartest thing to do, but it wasn't something I was really being rational about.

I believe that the crazy guy in today's passage and I had a lot in common. When I came to Christ, I had inner demons and Jesus had to kick them out of my life. Every time I went through that crazy stuff, I experienced total torment, but immediately afterward, I really did feel like something bad had been taken out of me. Christ delivered me, and after that season of intermittent madness was over—many months later—I had true spiritual strength. I could walk through almost any difficult circumstance without wiggin' out. I had become a new person, and now I can truly say I'm glad I went through that dark season, because it made me who I am today.

The crazy guy in Mark 5:15 got delivered, too. And after he did, our scripture passage says the guy was "sitting there fully clothed and perfectly sane," and all the people were afraid. Isn't it funny how a lot of our friends think we're weird and are afraid to come around us when Christ comes into our lives? Seems like it should be the other way around.

2 Corinthians 3:17

For the Lord is the Spirit, and
wherever the Spirit of the Lord is,
there is *freedom* [emphasis added].

If you're going through a lot of uncontrollable emotions because of inner pain, as I was, or if you find yourself in that place in the future, just hang on and never give up. I've been there and back. Maybe not as bad as you, but I've seen God be faithful in my life, and I know He'll do the same for you. It may look like He's not around, or like He's forgotten you, but He hasn't. Trust me. What you're feeling is just a part of the process to the road of true liberty. Stay on that road, and you'll never, ever regret it!

DAY 12

Exodus 33:18-19a (THE MESSAGE)

Moses said, "Please. Let me see your Glory."

God said, "I will make my Goodness pass right in front of you; I'll call out the name, God, right before you."

WHEN I WAS A KID, my family and I used to take long summer vacations in our motor home to see my dad's side of the family in Portland, Oregon, and Seattle, Washington. Sometimes the drives from California to Washington left us kids a little restless. My brother and I would really try hard to get along (and we actually did most of the time), but the cabin fever would eventually get to be too much and we would always end up getting into fights.

One summer we got into it so bad that my dad told us he was gonna pull the motor home over and let us fight outside until we were all bloody. He was only trying to teach us a lesson, of course—he wouldn't have let us rip each other apart—but at ages twelve and fourteen we did kind of wonder if he was serious. The picture in our minds of ourselves all bloody made us chill out the rest of the trip.

As I said, we normally did get along, and the thing that helped us keep the peace on those long journeys was knowing where we were going to end up. We loved to visit our extended family, especially since we didn't have a chance to see them very often. Our first stop would always be my dad's mom, Grandma Ruth. I have a lot of awesome memories of playing in my grandma's yard, eating her homemade jelly, playing in her basement, and just hanging around playing with cousins we rarely had a chance to visit with. Another fun thing we did on those vacations was go to the lake house of my dad's uncle, Uncle Harold. There was a boat at Uncle Harold's, so that's where I first learned how to water-ski. Another thing we once did at the lake house was ride in a helicopter over the lake. Man, that was a *huge* deal at age twelve!

I'm sure you can understand how looking forward to all of these amazing festivities at our destination really helped us sustain our patience on the long road trips in the motor home. Grandma, cousins, jelly, lakes, boats, and helicopters: a child's paradise!

Paradise . . . now that's a word that I love to meditate on. I like to chew on it over and over again in my mind and heart. And why not? After all, that's where God dwells. That's my destination. That's *our* destination.

Similar to the way my parents reminded us kids of what we could look forward to on our family vacations, God gives His true followers things to look forward to as we travel on the long road trip of life. He reveals beautiful glimpses of our destination to us at times and encourages us to look forward to paradise, where we will be saturated in the glory of His love, forever.

In our scripture passage for the day, God revealed His divine glory to Moses by passing in front of him. He does something similar for us, pouring a taste of His eternal paradise into our minds and emotions. In my experience, He grants these beautiful encounters just at the perfect time we need refreshing.

Oh man, do I love to feel God's glory pouring into my soul. There's nothing like it. It feels like rivers of peace surging into my emotions, flooding out all feelings of stress, anxiety, loneliness, sadness, anger, or anything else that may be affecting my life negatively. Just as it says in Exodus, every time I experience God's glory, all I feel is pure goodness. The peace in my heart is so intense that it feels like my soul is flying. Just wave after wave of divine peace.

Please ask God to help you experience His glory for yourself. I want so much for every person reading these pages to share this experience. It may take you a while to feel the intensity of His glory, as it did me; but if you ask and keep on asking, God will give you the desires of your heart. I'm telling you, there's nothing in this life that can compare to personally experiencing our heavenly Father's eternal glory. That experience has radically changed me: I'm not the same person I used to be. I still sometimes struggle in life, but God always lifts me out of my struggles and brings me back into His glory.

Every time.

If you want to experience God's glory, all that God requires is that you love Him above everything else in your world.

All you have to do is faithfully and consistently show Him that you do.

It's up to you.

DAY 13

1 Corinthians 2:9-12

That is what the Scriptures mean when they say, "No eye has seen, no ear has heard, and no mind has imagined what God has prepared for those who love him."

But it was to us that God revealed these things by his Spirit. For his Spirit searches out everything and shows us God's deep secrets.

No one can know a person's thoughts except that person's own spirit, and no one can know God's thoughts except God's own Spirit. And we have received God's Spirit (not the world's spirit), so we can know the wonderful things God has freely given us.

REMEMBER TRYING to read the Bible when I first became a Christian, and a lot of times it felt like I was reading an old history book. I couldn't get into it or understand it. That's when listening to sermons started to come in handy, because people who had searched out "God's deep secrets" over the years, or even decades, were able to share with me the truths that God had revealed to them. It's always good to listen to legitimate people teaching accurate sermons based on the Bible, because there are a lot of gifts for us inside other people. The gifts that God gives us are to *share*—not to keep for ourselves.

During the months after I first gave my heart to Jesus, I learned at a rapid pace because of all the sermons I listened to. Each talk helped me understand the Bible more. In addition, I learned how to pray in the Spirit (tongues), and that really sped up the process. Some days I would have to force myself to read the Bible, and other days I couldn't put it down. I started learning all about God's plan. From Genesis, with Adam and Eve, to Revelation, where God wraps up this whole plan of his (though I don't understand most of the book of Revelation even to this day!).

About two years after I gave Jesus my life, a really cool but unexpected thing started happening to me. It was a hidden gift from God that I received because He saw that I was seriously trying to learn about the history and facts of His plan in the Bible. *This is when things started to get very interesting and fun for me.* It was as if a door had opened in the spiritual realm and I started understanding what the Bible was saying about all the deep secrets God was giving me. I could really feel Jesus reading the Bible with me and helping me comprehend what everything meant by letting me experience the reality of the words:

1 John 2:27

But you have received the Holy Spirit, and he lives within you, so you don't need anyone to teach you what is true. For the

Spirit teaches you everything you need
to know, and what he teaches is true--
it is not a lie. So just as he has taught
you, remain in fellowship with Christ.

I get all fired up when I read that God's Spirit lives inside of me. Can you believe that? Have you ever thought about that long and hard and realized the truth of that amazing fact? It's completely mind-blowing, man! God actually lives inside of us and communicates with us. If you've already asked Christ into your heart, He's living in you, right now, as you read this. If you haven't asked Jesus to live inside of you, do it now. It's very simple. All you have to do is issue the invitation. I didn't mean to get off track, but I get really excited about the fact that the creator of the universe chooses to live inside of us.

Anyway, back when the doors of revelation opened up for me, the Holy Spirit taught me what the Bible meant as I was reading it, and all at once it stopped feeling like an old history book. Instead, it became a supernatural springboard that led me to encounter God for myself. I was experiencing Jesus similar to the way His disciples did. The feeling left me speechless.

Back then, when I read that God had raised us up with Christ and seated us in heavenly places (Ephesians 2:6), I could feel inside my heart that my inner spirit was actually somehow connected in heaven with Christ. When I read about God's unfailing loving-kindness, I could actually feel waves of love inside of me. When I read that I was in Christ and Christ was in me, I could feel the living Christ right then and there inside of my soul. It was all made possible by the Spirit of wisdom and revelation (Ephesians 1:17).

It says in Romans 4:17 that God calls things into being that haven't happened yet as if they *had* already happened. He has the power to do that, and that's how we can experience these things. He makes it so we can be connected with two realms at the same time—the earth realm where we live, and the spiritual realm where God is communicating to us from heaven. We live on earth, but we are also living in heaven, with God in our spirits and hearts. Likewise, God lives in heaven, but He also lives on earth inside of us. It's awesome!

Back when all this happened to me, I realized that God had begun to show me what today's Bible passage is all about: His deep secrets. Those are the most valuable gifts that any person can receive. The people who are blessed enough to discover these deep secrets are the richest people alive. Although the secrets are hidden from all of us at first, they are waiting to be discovered like a treasure. The map is the Bible, and the guide is the Holy Spirit.

Proverbs 25:2 (ESV)

It is the glory of God to conceal things,
but the glory of kings is
to search things out.

The Bible tells us that true followers of Christ are made kings and priests in God's kingdom. As we search out hidden meanings in God's word and gradually prove ourselves faithful in our relationship with Him, God begins to reveal the very things that were concealed from us. This is what God did for me. Now He's waiting to reveal His secrets to you when you search out His hidden gifts with your whole heart.

DAY 14

Hebrews 6:19-20a (NIV)

We have this hope as an anchor
for the soul, firm and secure. It
enters the inner sanctuary behind the
curtain, where Jesus, who went before
us, has entered on our behalf.

MOST PEOPLE BELIEVE that the human soul is made up of our mind, emotions, and will—in other words, our *thoughts, feelings,* and *actions.* When we merge our life with Christ, two separate souls are actually combined into one—our soul and the soul of Jesus. Our mind and Christ's mind come together, and suddenly the thoughts and words in our heads are no longer just our own. We experience our feelings along with Christ's feelings. Our actions and His actions are combined. The longer we work at developing our relationship with Jesus, the more the Holy Spirit will pour the likeness of Jesus into us so that we become "firm and secure" through any difficulty that comes into our lives. Is it easy to live firm and secure in Christ? No. Are we going to reach faith-perfection on earth? Of course not. Will we encounter

frustrations and questions along the way? Definitely. But with Christ we realize that we can "do all things through him who strengthens [us]" (Philippians 4:13, ESV).

In 1997, a friend of mine named Ron Vietti was living a normal, healthy life. He had a nice family and served as pastor of a big church that he and his wife had founded. Things couldn't have been better for him.

Then one day it all changed: he was diagnosed with leukemia and the doctors gave him three to five years to live.

Now, Ron was a man of great faith, but I'm sure he freaked out a little bit when the doctor gave him that news. Wouldn't you? *I* sure would. But after that freak-out, he went straight into prayer. Describing the experience years later, he recalled telling God that he really needed to hear something from Him about the situation. He prayed and worshipped the Lord nonstop, until one day he was totally positive that Jesus was giving him a verse: Psalm 91:7.

> Though a thousand fall at your side,
> though ten thousand are dying around you,
> these evils will not touch you.

Ron told his entire church that Jesus had given him a verse, and he invited everyone to watch him *not* die. A lot of people thought he was going crazy, or at least thought his ideas were not much more than wishful thinking.

To everyone's surprise but Ron's, through a series of miracles the leukemia vanished fairly rapidly from his body. Even though he is technically still diagnosed with the disease, doctors have not been able to detect signs of it in his body since 1998.

My point in sharing his story is this: when the words of those doctors were loaded onto Ron's back like a ton of bricks, he was very concerned, and he needed to hear from the Lord. He needed the hope that Hebrews 6:19 talks about in our daily passage; he needed that "anchor for the soul." When Jesus handed Ron Psalm 91:7, Jesus also gave him the faith that would make him "firm and secure"—no matter what the outcome would be.

Those words God gave him from the Bible allowed Ron's soul to experience unshakable faith and unshakable "hope" that took him into "the inner sanctuary behind the curtain, where Jesus, who went before us, has entered on our behalf." Many people believe that the "hope" this verse is talking about is our hope of going to heaven one day, after we die. That's true, but we need hope *as we live on earth* as well, especially when we go through heavy trials like Ron's. The "hope" that's mentioned in Hebrews 6:19 doesn't have the same meaning we usually give the word in our everyday language, which is along the lines of "I hope I don't die from leukemia." No, this passage is talking about a totally secure belief, one without a doubt. Faith is a real spiritual substance that makes us "sure of what we hope for and certain of what we do not see" (Hebrews 11:1, NIV).

There is a place we can get to in our faith where hope is pushed aside and total certainty of God's power to change things around for us takes over. When trouble comes our way, nobody has the final answer over our situation except the One who has already entered into heaven on our behalf—Jesus Christ, who lives inside of us.

Does that mean we can never struggle? Does that mean we can never for even a moment question God? Of course not, but God is big enough to take on all our pain and anger. It's important, though, to return again and again to the realization that God knows what He's doing.

"We have this hope as an anchor for the soul." If a ship's anchor is thrown into the sea, its heavy rope holding fast to the vessel, that anchor keeps the ship from moving even when rocked by a massive storm. It's the same with our souls. As we share one life with Christ (we in Him and He in us), the miracle of the secret relationship with Him is strength—strength to keep our peace and trust in Him anchored despite the storms of life.

Be certain of this: many storms will come into our lives. When they do, we may find ourselves reacting far from the way Ron Vietti did. But no matter our initial response, we must always remember that hard times can be used for our training. As I mentioned earlier, every difficulty builds our spiritual muscles, so that when we go through *future* difficulties, we'll be stronger. I for one can tell you that I'm able to walk through difficulties today that would've crushed me a couple years ago. I have been tested and tried repeatedly, and those trials have made me stronger than I've ever been in my life. Hard as it is to believe, difficult trials are actually *good* for us to go through: they help dig our anchor deeper into the sea-floor of divine love for a more firm and secure hold on the hope we have in Jesus.

DAY 15

Matthew 13:44-46

The Kingdom of Heaven is like a treasure
that a man discovered hidden in a field.
In his excitement, he hid it again and
sold everything he owned to get enough
money to buy the field. Again, the
Kingdom of Heaven is like a merchant on
the lookout for choice pearls. When he
discovered a pearl of great value, he
sold everything he owned and bought it!

THOUGHT ABOUT QUITTING KORN for at least two years before I made the final decision. At the time, I was involved
in real estate with some friends, and I was hoping to get
into a solid business relationship so that I wouldn't have to
worry about finances if I left the group. Money was one of
the main reasons I was afraid to quit Korn. I was depending
on wealth to keep me and my future safe and protected, but
my wealth couldn't buy me freedom from my drug addiction.
I tried paying to go to places that I thought could help me
get clean, but none of them worked. Likewise, when I first
started going to church, it was only because I thought maybe

the "Christians" could help me get clean. I was desperately looking for help from any human being who could do the job.

I didn't care who it was; I just needed to get clean.

The coolest thing about the church I ended up at—Valley Bible Fellowship in Bakersfield, California—was the advice Pastor Ron (the man who beat leukemia) gave people who were in trouble like I was. Ron encouraged everybody to get help directly from God. He said that Jesus was real and could help anybody with anything. After searching for a couple weeks, through prayer, scripture-reading, and conversations with people, I finally felt the reality of God's unconditional love pour into me. I was totally blown away by what I had discovered.

I suddenly understood that I had been depending on the wrong source for my security in life: my money. When I figured that out, I went through a season where I just wanted to get rid of my money, because I'd trusted in it for far too long. I wanted to flush my money out of my life as I did the drugs. I did have a desire to use it for God, but I also had a hatred for it; I didn't understand that *my love for the money* was what was wrong, not the money itself.

For the next four years, I gave my money away thoughtlessly and spent it foolishly, completely forgetting about the smart things I had done with it before I became a Christian. Sure, I'd wasted a fair bit on drugs, but I'd also worked hard to build up my financial security over the years. Now, though, having seen financial security for the weak anchor it is, I gave away my money to people I was connected with to invest in whatever they wanted to invest it in. I invested in my music quite a bit, too, but I definitely did so foolishly. I also invested in a food store, a meat packaging plant, a meat delivery business—all kinds of stuff that I knew nothing about. I wasn't even involved in running these businesses. I sold my house, gave money to the poor, moved to a state I'd never lived in before, and kept giving and giving and giving . . . until it was gone.

Looking back on it now, everything I did, I did to myself; God didn't do it to me. But I do feel like everything I went through was for a reason. I learned a lot through the whole process. I learned that God was always going to take care of me, no matter what mess I got myself into. I also learned that in spite of getting rid of my money like a fool, a lot of good came out of that divestiture. I needed to show myself and God that *He* was my provider from then on.

The parable in our daily passage in Matthew 13 talks about a man who got so excited about the treasure he discovered that he sold everything else he owned just so he could have what was most important to him. When I relate the parable to my own life, it makes me feel pretty good. Whether I was being an idiot or not by giving all my money away, I know that it touched the heart of God to see me let go of anything and everything I owned in hopes of getting as close to Him as I could.

Luke 18:22 (CEV)

When Jesus heard this, he said, "There is one thing you still need to do. Go and sell everything you own! Give the money to the poor, and you will have riches in heaven. Then come and be my follower."

Who knows, maybe some of the reason I've been able to experience such closeness to heaven since I've been a Christian is that I was able to let go of the riches of the earth. Isn't that what Luke 18:22 says? Again, so many people think that the scriptural passages about heaven deal only with when we die, but heaven is at hand, inside of us; and we're seated there with Jesus right now in the hidden recesses of our heart, even though our feet are on the ground. It's a supernatural reality that I've actually touched, so I know it's true by experience.

When God felt I was done showing Him that I'd give all my money away to have riches in heaven, He stopped me from being an idiot with my money and helped me out of the financial mess that I'd gotten myself into. It was all a faith-filled learning process for me.

Is there anything or anyone that you're holding on to for your security, as I was? Something or someone that you trust in more than God? Are you willing to let go of everything for the true riches in heaven? Ask God for strength to let go of anything that He thinks should go. This life is a walk of faith and obedience lived out through love from and for God. Anything that He asks you to let go of is for your own good—and trust me, He has riches from heaven that He will give you in its place.

DAY 16

2 Corinthians 5:18 (NIV)

All this is from God, who reconciled
us to himself through Christ and gave us
the ministry of reconciliation.

'VE BEEN TALKING with friends and family a lot about reconciliation lately. Wherever God is, you will see and hear a lot about people reconciling to Him and to each other. That's just who God is. He loves to restore things that are all but lost.

I have an old friend named D that many of you may remember reading about in my book *Save Me from Myself*. D helped me flush the last few eight-balls of speed I had down the toilet. He strongly encouraged me to go after God in the beginning. But then, around the summer of 2005, I moved out of Bakersfield and pretty much lost touch with D. It was mostly me who disappeared on him, though. I just needed to get away from my familiar old life and learn how to get close to the Lord.

Just recently, D's daughter, Alexis, showed up at a concert I did in Bakersfield, California. We talked for a few minutes after sound check and she told me her dad was in town. She

said he'd had other plans that night and hadn't been able to come, but I found myself hoping that we could connect some other time.

As it turned out, D had moved to Orange County not that long previously, and I actually had a show booked in Orange County a couple weeks after the Bakersfield show. When I learned that D was free to get together, I decided to take Jennea along with me to Orange County. D and his family had helped me take care of her after my ex-wife, Rebekah, and I divorced, and I was really excited for everyone to see each other again.

When we arrived in Orange County, we went to our hotel, and D and his family met us there. D, Alexis, and her brother, Torrie, got out of their car and saw Jennea standing up a level on the hotel walkway. As they walked toward her, a few tears began to flow. The last time they'd seen Jennea had been years earlier, when she was much younger. Just knowing what both our families had been through since then brought up some serious emotions in *all* of us. It was awesome to see all the kids together again.

The concert that I played in Orange County was at a place called the Sanctuary, which is a skate church in Garden Grove/ Huntington Beach. Pastor Jay, the senior pastor, is a skateboarder, and some other famous skaters (Christian Hosoi and Brian Sumner) are on the staff there, too. The church is filled with many people that look like me—which is to say, a bit freaky. There are a lot of tattoos around that church, for example. It's awesome.

Anyway, the show was crazy because it happened to be a special night: the Sanctuary has a reality show called *The Uprising* on the Inspiration Network, and they were premiering the second season at the church the night I performed. Jennea and D's family came onstage to watch the show from the side, and a cool thing happened before we played my song "Save Me from Myself." I shared with the crowd how D and I used to go around and party in Orange County after Rebekah and I divorced, and I admitted that we did some things around our kids that we shouldn't have—and then I apologized to the kids since they were right there. I started breaking down, and D and his family did, too. It was an intense and emotional night. We all ended up having a blast.

I've watched God totally reconcile so many relationships in my life. There was a season early in my faith-journey when I needed to go away and be alone, but when the time was right, I made the step back toward the important people in my life.

My experience with these acts of reconciliation is a big reason why the scriptural passage for today has meant so much to me. It's very important that we allow ourselves to be led by the Spirit through life. That's what faith is: giving God control of our lives because He loves us and knows what's best. I hope every one of you reading this will learn how to forgive and be forgiven. And when the time is right, you will be led back into the lives of the people with whom you desire to be reconciled.

DAY 17

Psalm 112:8a (NIV)

His heart is secure,
he will have no fear.

NOBODY EVER KNEW this about me, but when I quit drinking beer and doing drugs, I battled on and off with some of the same fears that had troubled me earlier in life.

In the beginning of 2005, a few weeks after I quit Korn, I did an interview with CNN at my house. Everything had shifted so fast for me. I was on fire for God, and my head was spinning from all the attention focused on me. For some reason, even though the CNN interview was going to be seen by millions, I wasn't nervous at all. I had the boldness to share my faith, and it was awesome.

But then, after I'd been with God for a while and my life had begun to calm down, I noticed some of my old fears starting to rise to the surface. For instance, I had an intense fear of public speaking and being in front of large crowds. I know: not a good thing when you're in the line of work I am. That was one of the reasons I partied so much over the years—to numb the fear and anxiety of being in front of large crowds.

Even though I was with God by that time, I still wasn't comfortable in my own skin. When I did public appearances, I was usually pretty calm if somebody else was interviewing me. When the time came for me to grab the mic to speak in front of people alone, though—that was a whole different story. I felt naked and exposed. Being in public is a lot different when you're drunk, playing guitar, and banging your head in a metal band than when you're standing in front of thousands of people sharing your life and pouring out your heart to them. I could no longer hide behind my guitar, my hair, or any alcohol or drugs. I was terrified.

One thing that helped me a lot during that time was the teaching of Joyce Meyer, whose books I turned to. Her message was simple: if you're scared to do something that you're supposed to do, then go and do it afraid.

Looking back on it now, the words seem so obvious, but that doesn't make them any less profound or influential. At that time in my life, I really needed to hear those words. After I took Meyer's advice to heart, I stopped worrying and started to trust God. The fears gradually melted away. I still had to face some fears every time I spoke in front of a large crowd, but each time I did, it got easier.

Being able to speak in front of crowds was important, but I was still only halfway there. I also had to overcome some nervousness about singing in front of people, because that was part of my new calling. Sure, I'd played guitar onstage for over ten years, but singing and being a front man was something totally different. When I first got my new band together, I was even terrified to sing in front of *them*. It was driving me crazy, but I just faced my insecurities head on and went and did it. And just as before, the fear melted away.

If you're reading this right now and you're battling with fear, I promise you that you will one day be fearless and secure if you invite God to go with you to face your battles.

Make the decision to face your fears with the Lord—no matter the cost. If I can do it, anyone can.

Joshua 1:9 (NIV)

Have I not commanded you? Be strong and courageous. Do not be terrified; do not be discouraged, for the Lord your God will be with you wherever you go.

DAY 18

Galatians 2:20 (CEV, AMP, NLT)

I have died, but Christ lives in me.
And I now live by faith in the Son of God,
who loved me and gave his life for me.

I have been crucified with Christ [in
Him I have shared His crucifixion]; it
is no longer I who live, but Christ (the
Messiah) lives in me; and the life I
now live in the body I live by faith in
(by adherence to and reliance on and
complete trust in) the Son of God, Who
loved me and gave Himself up for me.

My old self has been crucified with Christ.
It is no longer I who live, but Christ
lives in me. So I live in this earthly
body by trusting in the Son of God, who
loved me and gave himself for me.

BACK IN THE DAY, I went to incredible lengths to get my
drugs. I had two separate dealers, just to ensure access.
One lived in my hometown and the other lived a couple
hours away. Sometimes the local guy wouldn't return my calls

for days or weeks. This of course would make me incredibly angry; I'd call him over and over, leaving increasingly agitated messages on his answering machine. When I finally got him to bring some dope to me after one of these silences, he'd wave his shotgun around as he made the delivery—probably to send a message to me not to cross the line with him.

The other dealer was a friend of mine, someone I'd known for a few years. He was a pretty good guy, but like me he was wrapped up in the drug game (although from the other side). That dude and I would come up with some crazy stuff in order for me to have a supply of drugs while I was on tour. When I was going overseas, I'd try to pack enough drugs in my suitcase or gear to last until my return: I'd hide dope in vitamin pills; I'd take apart my deodorant and hide dope under the white stick, then put it back together; I'd take apart microphones or guitar pedals and hide the dope there.

One time I ran out of speed on tour overseas. After an emergency call from me, my dealer made a big candle and hid eight-balls of meth in the middle of it. Then he wrote me a fan letter, wrapped the candle up with the note as if it were a gift from a fan (in case Customs found it), and then posted it to Germany, where we were due to play. It was completely crazy tracking my package online, man—watching it stop in the UK and the Netherlands before finally reaching Germany. I wasn't sure if my eight-balls would arrive safely at my hotel room or if a bunch of police would charge through the door and take me to prison. It was definitely a stressful nightmare for me. Speed made me paranoid enough without all the crime I was involved in.

Then one day all of that changed. It simply died. I accepted Christ, and he came to live in me and give me resurrection power to put that old life to death and live a new life. Instead of looking for power through drugs and crazy dealers, I accepted the power of Christ. Instead of living in the crazy meth world, I began to live by faith in Christ. Instead of surviving on hidden drugs, I began thriving on the revealed power of my testimony.

When I was given the opportunity to go to Israel and get baptized in the Jordan River, I took it very seriously. I wanted to immerse myself in that water and show God and myself that I was completely dying to my old ways. I wanted to lay my old life down in the grave. That's what going down into the water to get baptized symbolizes: sharing in the death of Jesus and agreeing that you're going to take it seriously by putting your old self to death.

Being raised out of that baptismal water symbolized the resurrection that I was going to be living in my new lifestyle. But baptism didn't mean death to my old life and resurrection for my new life *on that day only;* it was like a spiritual contract between me and God that said I would be one with Jesus *from that day forward.* Being one with Jesus meant that I would have to live every day agreeing to die to my old ways, but also trusting in Him to give me new strength to overcome the trials in life. It also meant that I'd been given the gift to share in the resurrection power of Jesus. In other words, I was now able to take the power that I'd been given through Christ and pass it on—tell countless other people who were hurting like I was.

If you're at that same crossroads in your life right now, man, you gotta lay everything down and put your old self to death. Go and get baptized, whether it's in the Jordan or in your neighborhood church, and start living a new, resurrected lifestyle with Christ. Nothing else compares. It's a road filled with surprises that you don't know you're gonna get until you get them. Face it: no surprises await you if you continue down the same road you're on already.

If you live the same life you've been living, you're gonna get the same results you've been getting. Share in Christ's crucifixion, and you'll also get to share in his resurrection. The old you can be a memory, and the new you will be a beautiful thing. Everything in your life will be better.

Die to everything but God's will for your life. You can't share in the supernatural life on a deep level unless you give the things of the world over to the Lord. If you make that choice, you will truly be raised to a new, heaven-bound life in Christ.

DAY 19

1 Corinthians 6:16-17 (NASB)

Or do you not know that the one who
joins himself to a prostitute is one body
with her? For He says, "THE TWO SHALL BECOME
ONE FLESH." But the one who joins himself
to the Lord is one spirit with Him.

To *become one* with God. What does that mean? Well,
this verse seems to imply that it means a lot more than a
lot of us might think. Why is the speaker—Paul, one of
the earliest Christians—comparing a person being joined to
Jesus with a man being sexually joined with a woman? There's
got to be a message in here for us; this verse is in the Bible for
a reason.

I believe the verse is conveying a very deep message to us
about divine intimacy. My guess is that Jesus wants to be
joined with our spirit and soul in as deep a way as possible,
with sexual closeness being the most intimate union humans
can experience. The comparison is a sign, a picture, a parable,
and a message to believers. Jesus wants His passionate love to
flow out of His Spirit into ours, and from ours back to Him.
That's one of the reasons Jesus Christ died for us all. Jesus's

walk to the cross was the language of the heart. No words could speak it; only an *act* could truly do justice to the love of God shown in Christ.

I want to share an experience with you—an experience of soul "oneness" I had on January 19, 2007. But first, please read my disclaimer:

I've seen and heard of people being "slain in the Spirit," and it was totally weird to see people fall down and shake on the ground, crying or laughing their heads off. I kept telling God, "If that's *You* doing that, then I don't care how stupid I look: I want to be involved. I want to be closer to You."

Well, something crazy happened to me in the privacy of my own home, and these are the words I wrote that day. This passage is taken straight from my journal:

Jan. 19, 2007

> *I was reading 1 Corinthians 6 today for a while,*
> *while listening to worship music. As soon as I got to*
> *1 Corinthians 6:16–17, I felt the Holy Spirit's manifest*
> *presence in my body like never before. I felt like Christ*
> *walked right into me, and the reality of us being one in*
> *the Spirit completely overpowered and overwhelmed me;*
> *words cannot describe the feelings that I felt, but I guess*
> *I'll try.*
>
> *Instantly, tears began to well up in my eyes as I actually*
> *felt Jesus clearly speak these words to me: "We are one.*
> *These are my tears crying through your eyes." I began*
> *to shake. I felt the Lord looking through my eyes as the*
> *tears were gushing down my face like a river. These tears*
> *weren't drops like normal tears; they were streams that*
> *didn't stop for a long time. I was breathing heavily, as*

if the wind had been knocked out of me. I was trying to breathe normally, but it was very difficult. I just sat there in silence a while, in complete union with the Lord.

Whether I was caught up into heaven, or heaven was poured out into my soul, I don't know. All I know is that the complete oneness with the Lord that I felt was very real, and I knew I would never be the same. I ended up lying on the floor for a while in total contentment and peace. Since that day, the feeling has faded a bit, but I still have some of it in me to this day. It's as if Jesus imparted a piece of heaven into me.

I know, I know: this sounds kind of "out there." The truth is, it *is* weird to our human minds, but when God visits you like this, you're not really thinking about whether it's weird or not. I know *I* wasn't. Yes, it happened to me that day and I'm changed, but I'm not weird now or anything. I'm still basically the same guy I've always been. I haven't had an experience quite like that again yet, but I've had many similar experiences that were less intense.

That experience meant everything to me. Up to that point, I was still struggling every once in a while with wondering whether God was as real as I thought He was. After that intense encounter, all of my doubts disappeared forever. No joke.

If reading about my experiences makes any of you hungry to experience God like this, please know that He will give you deep encounters, too, if you thirst after Him more than anything on earth (Matthew 5:6). I'm gonna be real with you: I'm not trying to convince anyone that these things happened to me—in fact, I don't care if people believe me or not—but I want to share the wealth. The only reason I'm writing about these intimate things is because I want people to experience them for themselves—if they want to. However, it's important to understand that it's not enough to want to experience divine oneness just for the thrill of it. That's not what a life lived for Christ is about. This experience is not about thrills; it's about deepening your relationship with God in Jesus. Remember: no one person is more special than another to Jesus. He shows no favoritism. If your experiences differ from mine, that's cool.

Here are some of the things that I've done—and still do—to deepen my personal closeness to God:

1. Pray often, both normally and in tongues, if possible. (All kinds of people get too tripped out about tongues. It's more important *that* you pray than *how* you pray.) Get alone with God. Ask for experiences to happen every day until they happen. Practice quiet prayer. Meditate on God's love.

2. Read the Bible until you feel a scripture passage jump out at you and touch your heart, and then run the words through your mind over and over. When you feel it's time to move on, keep reading until something else touches your heart. You will feel the presence of God if you make a habit of this. And read other Christian books, too. I like to listen to good instrumental worship music while I read.

3. Spend as long as you can with God every day. The longer we spend with Him, the better we'll know Him.

4. Give up other pleasures that you know God is asking you to give up.

5. Do all of this out of love for Jesus, not out of desire for an experience. That's just icing on the cake.

When your experience of divinity does finally happen, you'll be rooted in the love of God so much that you'll feel as though you really are one with Him, as the Bible says we are (John 17:22). A lot of people say that it's not okay to seek after experiences with God, but that's not true; don't listen to that. A relationship with Jesus is like a marriage. You can let the passion fade away, or strive to keep the passionate love always burning. What would a marriage be like if the two in love didn't have experiences with each other? Pretty boring, right? And a relationship with God will get boring, too, if you don't experience each other. If we don't encounter the God who loves us, our relationship will be in danger of turning into boring, dead religion. So enjoy yourselves and have a blast going after experiences with God!

Colossians 3:1-3

Since you have been raised to new life with Christ, set your sights on the realities of heaven, where Christ sits in the place of honor at God's right hand. Think about the things of heaven, not the things of earth. For you died to this life, and your real life is hidden with Christ in God.

DAY 20

Daniel 12:10

Many will be purified, cleansed, and refined by these trials. But the wicked will continue in their wickedness, and none of them will understand. Only those who are wise will know what it means.

SO MANY CHRISTIANS, myself included, think that after God comes into our lives, we have to become perfect people. That, my friends, is religion talking. Religion is people trying to be good enough for God. The fact is, we *can't* act good enough for God because we don't know what's inside of us and we can't fix ourselves.

God desires Christians to achieve a certain level of maturity so that He can supernaturally purify, cleanse, and refine the inside of us. This is what today's passage says so eloquently—that a process of purification and refinement is essential for every Christian who means business. God does this by adversity, in the form of heavy trials that come into our lives over and over. According to a speaker I heard once, our emotions are the first objective of purification, because they are the most difficult to regulate (since they bypass the mind). From that starting point, the speaker said, the human soul-life must be tested (tempted and tried) time after time until Christians have confidence only in the soul-life of Christ in them.

Pretty deep.

Matthew 3:11 mentions the baptism of fire: a burning that comes inside of us when God allows adverse life episodes to burn out everything in us that doesn't live by faith. When negative situations come crashing down on us, our response reveals the true character that's inside our hearts. As various ugly aspects of that character rise to the surface each time we freak out and lose it in the middle of heavy trials, those aspects get taken out of us and replaced with the character of Jesus. I don't understand how, but our invisible God does this invisible work inside of us. Check this verse out:

Proverbs 20:30 (NIV)

Blows and wounds cleanse away evil, and beatings purge the inmost being.

As God allows these negative scenes to play out in our lives, these spiritual blows and wounds and beatings cleanse away the very things that we often pray that God will take out of our lives. Again, we can't change ourselves or conduct ourselves well enough for God. The Holy Spirit has to work the character of Jesus into our lives by refining us, as pure gold is refined under intense heat.

Revelation 3:18a

I advise you to buy gold from me--
gold that has been purified by
fire. Then you will be rich.

Jesus, in a vision reported by the apostle John in the book of Revelation, says in this passage that He desires for us to be purified by His secret ways of refining and cleansing through trials and tribulations. Gold symbolizes our faith, and the reality of the Holy Spirit purifies all of us who ask for it.

1 Peter 1:6-7 (NIV)

In this you greatly rejoice, though now for a little while you may have had to suffer grief in all kinds of trials. These have come so that your faith—of greater worth than gold, which perishes even though refined by fire—may be proved genuine and may result in praise, glory and honor when Jesus Christ is revealed.

Oh man, this stuff is so real! If you think you're ready for this, pray for God to bring His fire to purify you. You will start to experience very adverse circumstances, as I can attest.

I had been a Christian for about two years when I started praying for the Holy Spirit to bring fire into my life to refine and purify me. Finally, in February or March 2007, I started to feel like I was being refined and purified. Let me tell you, it was not fun, but it was necessary for me to go to a deeper place with God. God encouraged me during this period of refinement by giving me a lot of breaks in between the bad days. I often felt a heavy depression, along with a burning inside of my heart. I felt like screaming at God, and I cried a river over a few months. The darkness and gloom that came during the bad days brought so much confusion that I would forget that

I'd asked God to refine me; I'd just lose hope and break down all the time. But as I said, God did give me times of rest.

There was one book that helped me through the process: *Dark Night of the Soul* by Saint John of the Cross. He was a guy from the 1500s who went through the refining process in a major way and was gifted to write and teach about it. Never forget—this is all the process of a loving God doing what He does best: fixing us. God is called the Great Physician for a reason. He knows every hidden and dark area inside of us. His light and His light alone can search us inside to find and heal those things that are broken but hidden.

We all question God when we read scriptures that say Jesus will give us what we want if we ask in His name—we want to put Him to the test—but we should think about things before just praying. If we want to see our prayers answered right away, we need to start praying *unselfish* prayers (James 4:3). I suggest we pray for things that God would love to give us— things like purification in order to conform us to the image of Jesus.

Think about what I said earlier: after I started asking God for purification in early 2007, God actually started to purify me. Even after being a Christian for over five years, I still get excited at the fact that when I pray, God hears me and answers my prayers. I was excited when it happened back in 2007, too, even though the purification was painful. I was thrilled because it was little ol' me, one person out of billions, asking the God of the universe to do something—and He actually heard me and did it.

In general, I think that's something that we as Christians should get really excited about every day. Do you know how many people are out there who don't have what we have yet?

Listen, if you want to show God you mean business with Him, a prayer for purification or refining will show Him you love Him and you've actually laid down your life. God loves to give us the things we want and the things that make us happy, but there has to be a good balance. Love is a give-and-take relationship. Getting refined by God happens when we give our lives to Him as a sacrifice, as Jesus did. It's part of the giving side of our relationship with God. But when the refining is all over, we will learn that in giving ourselves, we received freedom from our loving God.

DAY 21

Acts 2:47b (ESV)

And the Lord added to their number day by day those who were being saved.

IT'S AN INCREDIBLE THING to see people's lives change direction right in front of your eyes. An amazing miracle to witness, it's yet more proof that Jesus is alive and everything He said is true. How can people's lives be changed so drastically? There's no other explanation but a miracle occurring deep inside of that person.

The most amazing, heart-changing miracles that I've witnessed are the ones where the person isn't looking for Jesus—Jesus just finds them, and changes their heart and life forever. It's just like the book of Acts says in our daily passage: every day people are finding God; every day the Lord is saving people. I've been stoked to witness quite a few of those transformations over the last few years.

In the summer of 2007, when my book *Save Me from Myself* was published, I did a book-signing tour all around the United States, and in my travels I heard all kinds of stories of faith from Christians old and new. Some of them were simple tales of how Jesus had found a person in a time of darkness, while others were dramatic tales of divine rescue. Mixed in with these, there were stories of some radically changed lives that completely blew me away. One guy came up to me at the end of a signing and began to ask me questions. He had an angry tone to his voice as he demanded to know how I knew for sure that God was real. I talked to him for a while and told him all about the changes that happened in my life.

This man began to share with me about his heavy drinking over the past few years. He said it had completely torn his family apart. He'd lost his job, and his wife had thrown him out of the house. He'd been literally walking the streets when he ended up in the bookstore where I was having my signing. He'd never even heard of me before. (I could tell he wasn't the type of guy who would've known about Korn.) After we talked for a while, I invited him back into an office and asked him if I could pray for him. As we were praying, he suddenly started crying—hard, wrenching sobs—saying that he needed God and wanted his family back. Through his sobbing, he prayed for Jesus to come into his heart and change him from the inside out.

After the prayer this man looked at me with a huge smile and kept saying how great he felt. He was grinning from ear to ear the whole time we talked after that prayer. Before the prayer, he'd had a dark look on his face, but all at once it had evaporated. Standing in front of me now was a new man— one who was filled with hope and couldn't wipe the smile off of his face.

In another city there was a big in-store signing with a line that lasted forever, or so it seemed. Toward the end of the line, this big ol' biker-looking dude came up to the table. He told me that he'd been praying a lot that one day I would come to his city and he'd be able to talk to me about what had happened to him. This guy wasn't a Korn fan at all. In fact, when he'd heard that I quit Korn and became a Christian, he had laughed and called me an idiot to his friends. Then, while he was drunk and high one day, he went to my website just for laughs—to make fun of the crazy rock star who thought he'd found Jesus. When he was on my site, he clicked on a CNN video of my testimony, expecting a few more laughs. As he was watching, though, his heart started to change, and he had the strongest feeling that he needed to find out what was in the book I was talking about in the clip: the Bible.

This guy *certainly* wasn't looking for Jesus. He was a prideful dude who was addicted to alcohol, drugs, and porn and had a dysfunctional home life and marriage. Despite all that, and his initial scornful attitude, he eventually found a church and became radically saved and changed by God. At first his wife thought he'd lost it—his change was that drastic—but after noticing that her husband wasn't going back to his old ways, she gave her life to the Lord as well. He also shared with me that his whole family had followed in his footsteps and given their hearts to Jesus. Just think about that: one guy, planning to make fun of me, not even looking for God, changed in an instant.

Another story is about a guy who came back from fighting in Iraq and got hooked on drugs and alcohol because of the things he'd gone through for our country. The postwar partying had taken its toll. He grabbed his gun one day and sat down on his couch to end it all. Something (or Someone) told him to turn on the TV. When he did, I was on TV talking about my freedom from drugs, thanks to Jesus. He decided not to end his life right then. He told his wife about it, and she eventually bought him my book. In short order his whole life was changed.

Another guy came to a club that my friend Ryan Ries rented out to use in following up with people who found God at a big Whosoevers event that I performed at in Las Vegas. This guy was walking by the club and decided to go in. He was on his way to kill somebody—I kid you not—but God led him into the club, and instead he gave his life to Christ that night! Afterward, the guy overheard someone else say that Jesus wasn't real, so he shared with the guy how he'd been going to kill someone earlier, but Jesus had stopped him. I wish I could have seen the look on the dude's face when he heard that!

There are so many stories like these that I guess I'll have to put a book out about them all one day. If you're a Christian, or you want to be, then dedicate your life and talents to Jesus and He will use you to change lives for the rest of your days on earth—just like He's doing with me.

There's nothing like the feeling of being used by God to totally change another person's life.

Nothing.

DAY 22

Isaiah 60:1 (AMP)

ARISE [from the depression and
prostration in which circumstances
have kept you--rise to a new life]! Shine
(be radiant with the glory of the Lord),
for your light has come, and the glory
of the Lord has risen upon you!

NEGATIVE CIRCUMSTANCES in life can cause deep depression. Shattered relationships, money problems, accidents—you name it—can drive us into an emotional pit. The negative circumstances that I had in my old life sent me into an emotional dungeon. When I first changed, it felt great to have peace in my life. All kinds of positive things happened to me. Then, after a few months as a Christian, God sent me some awesome spiritual gifts of wisdom that were wrapped up in a bunch of negative circumstances.

We've all heard the saying, When it rains it pours. In certain seasons, there's a lot of "rain" that comes into my life, bringing to the surface the negative attitudes inside me that need to die. A recent rainy day I had looked like this:

- Having a big fight in the morning with my daughter, Jennea

- Being nearly run off the road by a guy with road rage

- Getting served with a lawsuit

- Cutting my finger with a kitchen knife

And so on. All in one day.

But negative things are good for us once in a while, to mold our character into the image of God. Did Jesus have it easy?

Nope. Hebrews 5:8 tells us, "Even though Jesus was God's Son, he learned obedience from the things he suffered."

And so it is with us.

Before Christ enters our lives, negative circumstances seem to crush us to the point of despair and hopelessness. But God is trying to teach us some incredibly liberating lessons when he allows trials to come into our lives. Our daily Bible passage from Isaiah gives us a clue.

He wants to teach us how to *arise*.

That word "arise" says a lot. Remember: Ephesians 2 says that we are raised up with Christ and seated with Him in the heavenly realms. We have to learn to rise above our negative circumstances in life and live in peace, with our hearts at rest in heaven with Christ. No matter what we face, *God will help us through.* There's nothing that should be able to take that trust and confidence away from us. Sure, we get depressed and scared sometimes. We will always feel the pull and the pain of our daily struggles. Yet the ultimate reality in our lives is that we are with Christ right now, and God turns every bad circumstance around and makes good out of it (Romans 8:28). Can we actually learn to rise above our circumstances and live a life of peace and contentment, whether things are going well or badly in our lives?

Check this out:

Philippians 4:11-13

Not that I was ever in need, for I have learned how to be content with whatever I have. I know how to live on almost nothing or with everything. I have learned the secret of living in every situation, whether it is with a full stomach or empty, with plenty or little. For I can do everything through Christ, who gives me strength.

The key to our new lives with Christ is learning. Learning to trust God *always*. Instead of getting scared when our negative circumstances wrap themselves around our lives, we can learn from everything that comes our way. Paul, the apostle who wrote the passage just quoted, learned how to live on almost nothing by actually living on almost nothing and by drawing his strength from Christ to get through that negative circumstance. He also learned to live with wealth (which must have been a lot easier), but I would bet you that Paul was an extravagant giver when he was living large.

If you're going through negative things in life right now, arise and shine with the light of understanding that God is stronger than your circumstances. One of the best lessons that I've learned is to rest in love with Jesus, because He will miraculously turn everything around for you when it's time.

DAY 23

Luke 5:11

And as soon as they landed, they left everything and followed Jesus.

'VE BEEN TRYING to live my new life for many years now, but everywhere I go, every interview I do, everyone always asks the same question:

"Are you ever gonna go back to Korn?"

At first my answer was the same, simple response:

"Nope."

In 2007, when my autobiography, *Save Me from Myself,* was published, I made a point of apologizing to the Korn guys in the press. I admitted that I had said a lot of jacked-up things when I left in 2005. That started to make people ask more questions about a possible reunion. My answer gradually shifted from "Nope" to "I don't think so; I'm doing my own thing now."

Around that time, the Korn guys started mentioning to the media that they missed me, and a lot of the fans began to hope for a Korn reunion. Lead singer Jonathan Davis even said publicly in one interview that the door was open for me to come back anytime I wanted.

In 2008, when my first solo CD came out, a lot of people said my album reminded them of the earlier Korn days, and because of that, all of my post-CD interviews continued to raise the question of a possible Korn reunion. By that time my answer seemed to have shifted even a little more: "I can't say no for sure because you never know what the future holds. Never say never."

After a few years of my answers changing bit by bit, and the guys mentioning that they missed me, phone calls started coming from Korn's managers. When I was on a press tour in the United States for my solo CD, the Korn managers had people from their firm call the radio stations I was going to be at in L.A. to see what time I would be there. I guess they were trying to meet me face-to-face rather than going through my manager. It felt a little weird, but the people at Korn's management firm were really cool; they were only trying to make things work.

Since we felt a little awkward with Korn's people just showing up to my radio interviews, my manager contacted them on my press tour and asked them to call him directly to discuss things instead of showing up to my interviews uninvited. They agreed, phoning my manager promptly to ask what it would take to get me to go back to Korn. After my manager and I discussed it, we agreed that he would tell them that I had my solo career to focus on and we weren't interested. They were really cool with that and said okay.

That was it.

Then, in the summer of 2009, we discovered that Korn owed me a bunch of money from royalties on past Korn records that I hadn't gotten paid. No big deal. We worked with them for a couple months and they started making some payments. Then management started asking me to come back into the band again. They suggested offering me an opening spot on one of the Korn tours in 2010. I thought maybe that could be cool, but I just wasn't sure.

To be honest, all of these offers got my emotions churning. I started missing everyone in the band again. Then, in early 2009, Fieldy came out with his book about his faith, and I ended up calling him to offer my congratulations. We started texting each other a little after that, and one day he called me up to personally offer the Korn reunion to me. After the Korn managers asking me to rejoin the band many times, and now Fieldy, it made me wonder, "Am I running away from something that's meant to happen?" I told him I would pray hard about it.

I thought about how strong I felt when God led me out of Korn in 2005. Why would he want me to go back? Was I supposed to go back for just a short time? I wasn't sure, but after being offered the chance to open up before Korn's headlining spot, it started to seem like maybe it was meant to be.

But I still said no: I couldn't do it.

Until . . .

One day, I had an emotional meltdown onstage during a show when all my equipment messed up. I canceled the rest of the tour, got on a plane, and went to visit Fieldy. We talked about going to see Munky and Jonathan, our old colleagues from Korn, and hook up as friends. I left Fieldy's house and went to my favorite skate church, the Sanctuary in Huntington Beach, and prayed with pastor Jay that God's will would be done with the Korn meeting. An hour after we prayed, Fieldy called and said Munky and Jonathan didn't want to meet with me.

That was my answer.

After months and months of people talking about a reunion, the truth was that it wouldn't happen because it wasn't meant to be. But just before the last nail was hammered into the coffin, I heard that Munky did an interview telling people that I'd asked to rejoin Korn and they'd denied me. Calls came in to my publicist from people wanting to do an interview with me about getting "denied" by Korn. I couldn't believe he'd said that after a year of *them* asking *me* to come back. It's always possible, of course, that Munky didn't know the managers were asking me to come back all that time. I don't know. What I do know is that there are no hard feelings.

The coffin's nailed shut, though. That's the end.

Now I know without a doubt that *nothing* will ever convince me that I'm supposed to return to Korn. It's a done deal—100 percent never, never, *ever* gonna happen unless Jesus Himself appeared to me and told me to go back.

I'll close with this. If any of you have left everything in your life to follow Jesus as I did, then learn from my situation: there will always be temptations that try and confuse you to lead you back to the old, familiar life. Be reminded, though, that if you go back to the old, it's hard to walk by faith. "And without faith it is impossible to please God" (Hebrews 11:6, NIV).

DAY 24

Revelation 4:1-2 (CEV)

After this, I looked and saw a door that opened into heaven. Then the voice that had spoken to me at first and that sounded like a trumpet said, "Come up here! I will show you what must happen next." Right then the Spirit took control of me, and there in heaven I saw a throne and someone sitting on it.

CHRISTIANS WHO TALK ABOUT Jesus speaking to them and about other spiritual things often sound weird to non-Christians. I totally understand both sides. It wasn't very long ago that *I* thought Christians were weird. The whole faith thing looked like complete foolishness to me when I was on the outside, but my spiritual life with Jesus is everything to me now that I'm on the inside. I don't understand why it has to be like that. I love to share my faith with people because I can see and understand faith in the depths of my heart. But some people look at me like I'm crazy.

It's kind of frustrating.

Well, since I'm on the "weird" side now, I'm gonna get a little weirder and talk about the Spirit of God doing what He did to the apostle John in today's verse: "taking control" of someone and granting that person experiences with heaven.

The apostle John, who authored the book of Revelation, wrote about how he was taken by the Spirit to heaven even while his human body remained on the earth. His trip to heaven all happened in the spiritual realm. While John was in heaven, he walked around in his spiritual body—the form that he would later be given, after his natural body died and left the earth. Every one of us in Christ will be given a new, resurrected spiritual body when we leave the earth and go to heaven. Check it out:

1 Corinthians 15:42-44 (CEV)

That's how it will be when our bodies are raised to life. These bodies will die, but the bodies that are raised will live forever. These ugly and weak bodies will become beautiful and strong. As surely as there are physical bodies, there are spiritual bodies. And our physical bodies will be changed into spiritual bodies.

Please allow me to make a point here. I totally honor all of the people in the Bible, but they have all left the earth and are with God now in their new spiritual bodies. Who does that leave to get to know God in the ways that the people in the Bible did *before* they died?

You and me.

There are so many regular men and women in the Bible that God revealed Himself to in crazy, spiritual, supernatural ways. From Abraham, the father of faith in the Old Testament, to the apostle Paul in the New Testament—the guy who okayed the murder of Christians before he met the resurrected Christ. If a murderer of Christians can know Jesus in such an intimate way by encountering heaven in the spiritual realm, then maybe we should all really consider how close we are to Jesus in our lives today. Could we be missing out on more?

I've had the privilege of knowing God better. I mentioned earlier about an ecstatic ride I had with the Lord in January 2007. The Holy Spirit took control of me and allowed me to experience a glimpse of the eternal afterlife promised me through Jesus.

Some of you may be thinking, "What's this guy talking about? How can he say he experienced heaven?" I'm not telling you this for you to think special of me. I'm sharing my spiritual experiences in hopes of creating a spiritual hunger in you to go after God with everything you have. It trips me out that so many people, especially even some Christians, think it's crazy talk to have experiences with heaven. I mean, we humans have invented the phone and Internet to speak to other people or send messages to them on the other side of the world in a matter of seconds, but we don't believe God can contact us in intimate ways?!

That's like saying we're smarter than God. Now *that's* crazy talk! How can I call or send an e-mail to China in a matter of seconds, but then say Almighty God can't take control of me with His Spirit and show me the heavenly realm?

It doesn't make sense.

Our disbelief comes from pride. We've gotta kill our pride, man. Now, I'm not saying I have crazy encounters like I did in

January 2007 all the time or whenever I want. They're granted to Christians by God, *when He wants and how He desires.*

If you reject the idea that I'm a crackpot and instead choose to believe that God is smarter than humans and can communicate with us however He chooses, then you're on the road to knowing God better—maybe even experiencing heaven on earth.

If you don't believe what I'm saying or you're not into going after God with all your heart in order to know Him more, then a couple things will happen for sure:

1. God will love you no matter what.

2. As soon as you die and enter the spiritual realm, you're gonna understand everything I'm saying, and as soon as you cross over into eternity you'll say to yourself, "Damn! I shoulda listened to that tattooed guy when I read his book. I missed out on a lot!" I say this in hopes of making your desire for Jesus increase. I know the Lord, and there's nothing that He'd want more than to have you believe He can do what He says He can do.

To all you ex-druggies who are questioning all this—remember how you used to snort up lines, shoot your veins up, or suck on pipes for hours to get high? You went to crazy lengths to experience serious highs back then. I want to challenge you to stay crazy, like you used to be, but instead of chasing drugs, chase God. Let His Spirit take control of you. Living life in such close proximity to Christ is the best high you'll ever have. And to all the conservative people reading this: there's so much more of God to go after, so come and join us and go after God with everything that's in you.

Believe and you shall receive.

DAY 25

Isaiah 41:14-15

Though you are a lowly worm, O Jacob, don't
be afraid, people of Israel, for I will
help you. I am the Lord, your Redeemer.
I am the Holy One of Israel. You will
be a new threshing instrument with many
sharp teeth. You will tear your enemies
apart, making chaff of mountains.

THE NIGHT I PLAYED my very first solo concert was close
to the four-year anniversary since I had played my last
show with Korn. I was ready to get things rocking again,
so a lot of preparation went into that show. A friend of mine
named Jeremy had set up the show at a place called Phoenix
First Youth Pavilion. He and his wife, Roxanne, were putting
on a weekend event, and I was just one of the guests invited
to perform. Tim Maiden from Church for the Nations helped
Jeremy and Roxanne put the event together. Skateboarder
Brian Sumner came and shared, and a rapper named the Rep
gave an awesome performance.

Everything came together quickly for the event. My band
had just been formed when the invitation came—I'd barely
started to sing in front of people, and we had only three weeks

to rehearse for the concert. I felt like the lowly worm Isaiah talks about in our daily passage—scared and insecure. I was unsure of my voice and unconfident about my role as the front man. Furthermore, I was overwhelmed with anxiety about performing in front of a crowd again. I felt ready to rock and ready to quit at the same time. Yes, I was a total worm, but I just kept moving forward. Joyce Meyer's special words, quoted earlier, helped me: "If you're afraid to do something, then go and do it afraid." As long as I kept moving forward, I knew God would show up—but I still felt like a worm.

Jeremy is an all-or-nothing kind of guy, and he wanted to fly me and my band to our first show in a helicopter. At first I wasn't into the idea, because it reminded me of a Bon Jovi entrance or something; but Jeremy kept pushing, so I went ahead with it. The night of the concert was a trip, man. My new band members—Michael Valentine, Scott Von Heldt (SVH), Dan Johnson, Ralph Patlan (Skeemo), and Brian Ruedy—played Rock, Paper, Scissors to see which two would go on the helicopter with me. Skeemo and Ruedy won.

When we got to where the 'copter was, we met the owner and pilot, Mitch. Man, what a cool guy! He had all these great cars and a helicopter, but from the first moment we met him he talked about the Lord and said how all his "toys" were nothing compared to Jesus. When we took off, I was a little nervous. Mitch's helicopter had been built to film movie scenes, so it had great visibility: we could see out of the 'copter from the "ceiling" almost to our feet. It felt as if we were floating in the sky. I told Mitch about a dream I'd had a few days earlier about floating in the sky and pointed out that the helicopter experience was pretty much that dream coming true.

We flew around the Phoenix/Scottsdale mountains for a while and then headed to the concert. When we approached to land, we saw a big crowd of people waiting in line; we could also see all the security and event people below us. By the way, I was totally right about Bon Jovi. It did feel just like a Bon Jovi entrance getting out of that 'copter, but it was awesome. We shook some people's hands in line and then went inside to get ready for the show.

Minutes before the show, I felt so nervous that I had a hard time breathing right. I'm sure you're wondering how I could be so nervous about playing in front of people after having been in Korn for so many years. As I said before, playing guitar drunk is a lot different than playing guitar and singing as the front man in concert while totally, stone-cold sober.

I felt like that lowly worm again before I walked onstage, but as we played the first song—a number called "Adonai"— I could feel myself being transformed from a worm into a "threshing instrument." It was a short set, but I got to share with the crowd about the transformation that had taken place in my life. Jeremy had bused in a bunch of kids who lived on the streets, and it was awesome to see them all get touched by God and receive Christ into their lives.

On that day, God changed me yet again. He keeps on changing me, and He'll change *you* if you let Him. If there's one thing I've learned about God, it's that He'll lead you to face your fears if you're willing, because He doesn't want any of us to be a slave to fear.

Romans 8:15

So you have not received a spirit that makes you fearful slaves. Instead, you received God's Spirit when he adopted you as his own children. Now we call him, "Abba, Father."

I encourage you to face your fears head on—even if you feel like a lowly worm, as I did. God can transform you into a fierce threshing instrument, too—and you'll never be the same.

DAY 26

Psalm 139:3-4 (CEV)

You notice everything I do
and everywhere I go.
Before I even speak a word,
you know what I will say.

MANY PEOPLE THINK that you have to give up all the fun in life when you become a Christian. What really happens is that you put down temporary pleasures and in turn pick up real pleasures that last forever. It's an indescribable feeling. An experience impossible to put into words.

Psalm 139, from which our daily verses are taken, was written by King David, who (the Bible says) was a man after God's own heart. What David wrote in this psalm was a personal revelation that he'd received from God. I've noticed over the years that God gives His children intangible things that are very personal—both to Him and to us. Some of the things, like this revelation to David and the feelings of love and intimacy God gives me, are so personal that a person's soul feels saturated with God's love. Kind of like the feeling that two lovers share when they're completely oblivious to the outside world.

God doesn't do this with everybody, though—only the people who are done with the world and are willing to do anything to know him personally. The favors and delights that God gives to these souls are unexplainable. They far outweigh any pleasure on earth—anything from filling your stomach with the tastiest food and drink to enjoying erotic pleasures. *Nothing* compares to divine pleasures.

Psalm 139 was a personal letter from David to God, but just like any scripture in the Bible, every word written in that psalm is for anybody who searches. The Holy Spirit gives us the living words of the Bible and deposits them in our hearts—a little bit in the beginning of our relationship and a lot later on, as we prove that we aren't gonna throw in the towel when things get hard. When the Holy Spirit's deposits take place, the words we are given are poured into our souls like liquid love.

One day, as I sat and read Psalm 139, I felt God lead me to do a paraphrased version of the first eighteen verses—told from God's perspective rather than from David's, as in the original—which I have shared with you below. These words are what God revealed to me that day. They were very personal to me, and I hope they become very personal between you and God right now, too.

Read these words slowly and many times over. As you do all this, directly apply the incredible truths offered here to yourself. Insert your name if that helps. Do whatever you need, because every promise in the Bible is for *everyone* who believes. All you have to do is ask God to make these words real for you.

I have looked deep
into your heart,

and I know all about you.
I know when you are resting
and when you are working,
and from heaven
I discover your thoughts.
I notice everything you do
and everywhere you go.
Before you even speak a word,
I know what you will say,
and with my powerful arm
I protect you from every side.
I know you can't understand all of this!
Such wonderful knowledge
is far above you.
There is nowhere you can go to escape
from my Spirit
or from my sight.
If you were to climb up
to the highest heavens,
I would be there.
If you were to dig down
to the world of the dead,
I would also be there.
Suppose you had wings
like the dawning day
and flew across the ocean.
Even then my powerful arm
would guide and protect you.
Or suppose you said, "I'll hide
in the dark until night comes
to cover me over."
But I see in the dark

because daylight and dark
are all the same to me.
I am the One
who put you together
inside your mother's body,
and you are wonderfully made,
the way I created you.
Everything I do is marvelous!
Of this you should have no doubt.
Nothing about you is hidden from me!
You were secretly woven together
deep in the earth below,
but with my own eyes
I saw your body being formed.
Even before you were born,
I had written in my book
everything you would do.
My thoughts are far beyond
your understanding,
much more than you
could ever imagine.
If you try to count my thoughts,
they would outnumber the grains
of sand on the beach.
And when you awake,
you will find me nearby.

DAY 27

Romans 12:3

Because of the privilege and authority
God has given me, I give each of you this
warning: Don't think you are better than
you really are. Be honest in your evaluation
of yourselves, measuring yourselves by the
faith God has given us.

THE INITIAL TOUR we booked for my first solo album was through New Mexico, Colorado, and Texas. After the amazing first show we played in Arizona, the band and I were ready to hit the road and experience many more incredible shows. I figured that, since I was from the band Korn, and Korn typically had thousands of people showing up at their concerts, we would have no problem bringing in at the very least 250 to 300 people.

The first stop on the tour was Colorado Springs. Everything seemed great when we arrived there. A local radio station was spinning my single "Flush," and we had an interview on the morning radio show that I thought went pretty well. Later in the day, we had sound check, and it went off without any problems. I headed back to the hotel, got ready for the show, then hurried back to the club—actually, a bar with a cool stage—to get things started. When I walked out to play, my heart sank. Fewer than a hundred people were crowded in front of the stage; behind them it was empty all the way to the back of the club.

Well, it wasn't exactly empty *all* the way back. There were some people sitting at the bar and a few people playing pool. That kind of made it worse, though, because the people at the bar and playing pool were conversing as if we weren't even there! I guess I'd been thinking too highly of myself when I thought "the guy from Korn" could at least pack out a bar. Don't get me wrong, I appreciated the fans that were there; but it was a hard adjustment to go from playing in front of huge crowds to seeing an empty place. It made me feel like I sucked. It's the dread of every famous musician—that your crowd disappears and doesn't care about you anymore.

The show went great, though. The people who were there were really into it, and after the show, the band and I got to talk to them. That was something that rarely happened when I was with Korn. A lot of them said we sounded better than our album, so we were stoked. After the show, an amazing thing happened. We learned that a girl named Michelle, who had been diagnosed with breast cancer, had driven out from Minnesota to meet us, because she wanted us to pray for her. When we heard that, we invited her into the back lounge of our tour bus to pray together. In the Korn days, the back of the bus was known for many things, and *none* of those things was praying. So it was an amazing thing to lay hands on a girl to pray for her, rather than laying hands on her for other, obvious reasons like the old days.

The next night, we played in Farmington, New Mexico. There were more people at that show, and everyone was going crazy. I had my first encounter with a drug dealer on the road at the Farmington gig. Some dude came up to me and asked if I wanted to buy some dope. I calmly told him no thank you. Drugs simply aren't tempting to me anymore. To me it's like someone saying, "Hey bro, do you wanna buy a piece of crap?" That's what drugs are, so why would I want to buy poop?

Ultimately, the mix of those first two stops on the tour continued for the whole summer. We played some horrible places that were empty, and we played some huge places that were packed. For the smaller gigs, I tried to adjust to the fact that I was starting all over again, which meant paying my dues all over again. At the beginning of the tour, I'd thought I was above having to start from scratch because I was from the mighty rock band Korn. But God has a way of smacking you back down to reality; it's called humility.

That summer, I had a couple really heavy emotional meltdowns that sent me running away and throwing in the towel, but God never let me go. I was definitely humbled and taught to reevaluate myself honestly. The biggest lesson I learned was that my satisfaction and contentment don't come from playing tiny shows that look like failures, or huge shows that look like successes. They come only from my relationship with Jesus.

The next time you find yourself running around feeling unsatisfied because you don't appear to have everything you want at that moment, remember that everything you really want and need is already living inside of you, and His name is Jesus.

DAY 28

John 14:14 (ESV)

If you ask me anything in my name,
I will do it.

EVER SINCE I WROTE ABOUT my ex-wife, Rebekah, in my book *Save Me from Myself,* a lot of people have told me they've been praying for her and want to know how she's doing. I mentioned in that book that Jennea and I got to pray with Rebekah when we visited with her in Hawaii in 2005. For a while after that Rebekah did very well, and we even talked about Jennea living with her in Hawaii for a certain amount of time. Unfortunately, that never worked out, and a few times now Rebekah has fallen back into her old ways. The drugs were too tempting in the environment she was in. When she did drugs, she turned into a different person—as we all do.

Watching her go through this struggle was hard for me. I wanted so much for her to be released from her addictions, but each time she returned to drugs, I felt myself becoming increasingly cynical about her ability to pull away from them. I was frustrated with her, but truthfully, I wasn't thinking enough about my faith as I looked at her situation. I was quick to criticize and quick to judge, and I gave up believing that God would do something good in her life. Simply put, I thought Rebekah was too far gone to turn around.

I've since learned that kids are a lot smarter than adults sometimes.

Jennea knew that her mom was having trouble. She started praying for Rebekah almost every night before bed. She prayed that her mom would stay off drugs and have a happy life. God wants us to have faith like a child, but I didn't have much of anything for Rebekah.

I've seen so many prayers answered by asking Jesus for things in His name, as He says to do in John 14:14. Some of the prayers that I've mentioned to God haven't happened yet, but I know He heard me and will answer them in the right way and in His time. No prayer has ever fallen from God's ear that has been prayed in the name of Jesus, and that's what Jennea was doing almost every night for her mother. Night after night she'd pray for Rebekah's health and happiness and her ability to make good decisions. Usually while Jennea was praying, I would think to myself something like, "Good luck with *that* one, God."

For the first time in a long time, I had weak faith.

As the time passed, Rebekah gave birth to another daughter, named Alanna, and the only thing I believed was that Rebekah—despite this wonder of new life—was going to do the same thing she'd done before: fall back into her old ways. I wasn't trying to be negative and I did pray for a miracle for her, but I was just so frustrated. Frustrated because for so long my prayers for Rebekah had gone unanswered. Frustrated because Rebekah seemed so incapable of facing her demons. Frustrated because I wanted my daughter to be able to have a mom I could trust: I wanted Jennea to be able to visit her mom by herself, for both their sakes, but I couldn't allow that to happen until I saw proof that Rebekah was doing well. I'm happy to say that the proof finally came.

At the time of this writing, Rebekah has been working (sometimes two jobs) and raising Alanna for over two years. She seems stable and happy, and I'm really proud of her. I'm also proud of Jennea for believing that God heard her prayers and would be able to do what oftentimes looked impossible. The best part of all this: I bought Jennea a plane ticket to go and see her mom by herself for the first time in many years. (Jennea was eleven by then, and she was used to flying by herself a few times a year—usually to meet up with me someplace on tour or to visit my parents.) Since Rebekah was doing so well, I felt it was time to take that next step. And the first trip went amazingly well! They stayed in a nice hotel in Lake Tahoe. Rebekah took Alanna and Jennea up to play in the snow, and they all went sleigh-riding. Jennea told me they laughed pretty much the whole time.

When it came to Rebekah, Jennea had the faith that I did not, and God used her to show me that I had been doubting Him, even though I hadn't meant to. You and I can both learn from Jennea. If you don't see results from your prayers right away, keep praying. We shouldn't give up so easily.

Also try to learn from me. Try not to be an idiot and doubt as I did. If you ask for anything in the name of Jesus, Jesus will do it. I'm not talking about asking him to let you win the lottery or for a hot girl or guy to ask you out; I'm talking about prayers that touch his heart. Prayers like Jennea prayed about her mother. Prayers about growing closer with Jesus. Prayers that are unselfish, as we saw earlier. James 4:3 says, "You ask and do not receive, because you ask with wrong motives, so that you may spend it on your pleasures" (NASB).

I've seen all kinds of prayers answered by God; however, these examples are dedicated to my faith-filled daughter, Jennea, who I can always count on to get my back when my faith runs out.

DAY 29

Philippians 3:10-11

I want to know Christ and experience the mighty power that raised him from the dead. I want to suffer with him, sharing in his death, so that one way or another I will experience the resurrection from the dead!

I HAVE A STRONG DESIRE to learn about suffering while I'm here for this short stay on earth. Not normal suffering, but suffering with Jesus. Why? Because I've been through many, many difficult things since being a Christian, and I want to understand why so I don't become a bitter person. There are a lot of people who have experienced way heavier things than me, like a death in the family, martyrdom, or something of that magnitude. Sometimes I feel like I'm being a wimp, but there's no doubt in my mind that I've gained a lot of spiritual knowledge by persevering through the things that have tried to knock me down and out.

There have been times when I've said to the Lord, "Are you for me or against me?" As obvious as the answer is to that question, at times it's been difficult for me to see it. That's how hard things have been. In those times, I've felt everything from being frustrated to being offended. I've kept asking, "How could God allow this to happen to me?" But those experiences have led me to some very deep spiritual truths about suffering with Jesus and sharing in His death.

The disciples who walked with Jesus really found out what "sharing in His death" meant. They walked to their own deaths, just as many Christians in other countries today suffer actual torture and death. And all because they confess the name of Jesus! They are true heroes. Still, this is *my* life, and I've suffered a lot in my own ways; in my own ways, I've shared in Jesus's death by giving up my former life that I chose for myself. When I was rich and famous, everything was great on the outside, but my inner life was often a torturous dungeon. Nowadays my inner life is great, but sometimes my outside life has been very shaky, to say the least. I like to talk with people about the trials I've gone through to help them understand why *every* Christian must face his or her own set of difficult circumstances to suffer with Jesus.

Let me just say this first: I believe that one of the most important things God wants to accomplish in our lives is having Christ become formed inside of us. But many people who become Christians don't really understand that they actually share one life with Jesus Christ. One of the goals in sharing one life with Christ should be immovable inner strength. With Jesus Christ actually living inside us, we should achieve so much inner strength that we're eventually able to walk through any external turmoil or chaos while staying in peace and trust on the inside. The ability to hold our negative emotions and thoughts at rest while life's storms are raging all around us is a sign of true spiritual maturity. One of our main goals as Christians should be the desire to develop a high threshold for pain.

2 Corinthians 1:5-6

The more we suffer for Christ, the more God will shower us with his comfort through Christ. Even when we are weighed down with troubles, it is for your comfort and salvation! For when we ourselves are comforted, we will certainly comfort you. Then you can patiently endure the same things we suffer.

When Jesus was hanging on the cross for us, fiercely beaten and pierced by nails, He bled and died a painful death for us to be saved and comforted by God. Likewise, Jesus was also saved and comforted from *His* pain and death by God when He was resurrected.

As we are weighed down with troubles in our lives nowadays, the difficulties act as a spiritual cross that we carry for Jesus (Luke 9:23). We are often spiritually beaten, and we sometimes feel as though we are bleeding and dying emotionally. But as we endure these difficult trials, God delivers us out of them, comforts us, and turns the scars that remain into spiritual badges of honor—just as He did for Jesus. We are then gifted and anointed to help others. Again, just like Jesus.

This is how we share in the death and resurrection of Jesus, the experience that our daily passage from Philippians is talking about. Because we share one life with Jesus, we are no longer living for ourselves without any purpose. Every time we suffer by going through trials and every time we are resurrected out of them, we are living out God's plan for us to share one life with Jesus. If we are "married" to Jesus in His afflictions, we will be "married" to Him in His resurrection—not only when we die, but spiritually speaking; in other words, we will experience death and life over and over again through life's circumstances as we walk with Jesus on the earth.

In Colossians 1:24, the apostle Paul said that he was glad when he suffered in his body because he understood how every Christian has a participating role to play in the sufferings of Jesus that continue for *his* body, the church. But Paul also understood the other side of suffering—the side that comes immediately *after* we suffer, bringing ear-to-ear smiles to our faces:

Colossians 3:1-4

Since you have been raised to new life with Christ, set your sights on the realities of heaven, where Christ sits in the place of honor at God's right hand. Think about the things of heaven, not the things of earth. For you died to this life, and your real life is hidden with Christ in God. And when Christ, who is your life, is revealed to the whole world, you will share in all his glory.

We share in Jesus's glory when we die, and we share in his glory every time we suffer in this life. We have to let God build our faith to experience his glory now on earth—not just in heaven after we die. The Bible says we've already died and are already raised to new life. While I believe that *most* days, I wish I could live in that truth when I'm going through trials. The fact is, even though deep down I live in peace and trust, I usually get in a bad mood when I go through suffering, and I end up acting like the old me rather than someone who has already been "resurrected to new life." I'll get there one day, though, and so will you.

When you're going through suffering, Isaiah 53 is a great chapter about how we share in the sufferings of Jesus. It's about Jesus's crucifixion and resurrection:

Isaiah 53

Who has believed our message? To whom has the Lord revealed his powerful arm? My servant grew up in the Lord's presence like a tender green shoot, like a root in dry ground. There was nothing beautiful or majestic about his appearance, nothing to attract us to him. He was despised and rejected--a man of sorrows, acquainted with deepest grief. We turned our backs on him and looked the other way. He was despised, and we did not care.

Yet it was our weaknesses he carried; it was our sorrows that weighed him down. And we thought his troubles were a punishment from God, a punishment for his own sins! But he was pierced for our rebellion, crushed for our sins. He was beaten so we could be whole. He was whipped so we could be healed. All of us, like sheep, have strayed away. We have left God's paths to follow our own. Yet the Lord laid on him the sins of us all.

He was oppressed and treated harshly,
yet he never said a word. He was led
like a lamb to the slaughter. And as a
sheep is silent before the shearers,
he did not open his mouth. Unjustly
condemned, he was led away. No one cared
that he died without descendants, that
his life was cut short in midstream.
But he was struck down for the
rebellion of my people. He had done no
wrong and had never deceived anyone.
But he was buried like a criminal;
he was put in a rich man's grave.

But it was the Lord's good plan to crush
him and cause him grief. Yet when his
life is made an offering for sin, he
will have many descendants. He will
enjoy a long life, and the Lord's good
plan will prosper in his hands. When
he sees all that is accomplished by
his anguish, he will be satisfied. And
because of his experience, my righteous servant will make it possible for
many to be counted righteous, for he
will bear all their sins. I will give
him the honors of a victorious soldier,
because he exposed himself to death. He
was counted among the rebels. He bore the
sins of many and interceded for rebels.

As we mature in our calling, we will share in His sufferings more and more. Rest assured, we will sometimes feel like we are "despised and rejected, a man of sorrows, acquainted with grief, oppressed and treated harshly, unjustly condemned, struck down." But, like Jesus, we will also be raised up to experience the heavenly realms, and we'll be totally satisfied by the countless lives that God helps change through us.

DAY 30

Psalm 91:14 (ESV)

Because he holds fast to me in love,
I will deliver him;

I will protect him, because he
knows my name.

SO MANY OF US RUN AROUND and try to do things for God when all God wants is one thing: our love. This is the one thing the Lord desires above all else. How much does He want us to love Him? Let's try and figure it out.

Genesis 2:24 talks about how Adam and Eve, both naked in the Garden of Eden, were joined together as one in the first union between a man and a woman: "Therefore a man shall leave his father and his mother and hold fast to his wife, and they shall become one flesh" (ESV). "Holding fast" and "becoming one flesh" with another person means achieving complete spiritual, emotional, and sexual intimacy. In our daily verse, Psalm 91:14, God is talking about a person who "holds fast" to Him in love. See the similarities?

The Bible clearly says that Jesus wants us to love Him until we are so close that we become one spirit and one heart with

Him, like a bride and groom. After all, that's what we, the church, are to Christ—his bride. Odd to picture myself as a chick, but being the "bride of Christ" represents exactly what we're talking about: deep, rich, true love.

That's just one picture of God's desire for intimacy. There are many different examples and pictures in the Bible of how God desires us to love Him. His love is so much deeper than our limited human understanding, and yet it's so simple. But we humans always complicate things.

Some of you are probably thinking, "God wants us to *do* certain other things, too." I totally agree, but if we love God with severe intensity, everything we do will be saturated with His love. Love for God is our starting point. When our love for God in Christ is laid as the primary foundation, we won't need to strive to do things for Him. Instead, God's Spirit will flow through us intimately yet powerfully, encouraging us to work *with* Him.

Matthew 22:37-39

Jesus replied, " 'You must love the Lord your God with all your heart, all your soul, and all your mind.' This is the first and greatest commandment. A second is equally important: 'Love your neighbor as yourself.' "

God desires us to love Him with all our heart and all our soul because He loves us with all His heart and soul. God wouldn't ask us to do anything that He hasn't done first. If we stay connected with God in love, as He desires, scripture says we will be delivered and protected from life's difficulties. That doesn't mean difficulties won't happen; they will, and as I talked about in earlier reflections, we'll be stronger for them. What it *does* mean is that we'll never be alone in our troubles. And we'll be rescued and honored and be saved from every hole that life throws us in.

Perhaps you just started your relationship with God, and you're feeling confused about all of the potential ways that you could work to spread the love of Him. Or perhaps you're a seasoned Christian struggling with the anxiety of feeling like you need to be doing much more than you are for God. Either way, the lesson is the same: your task first and foremost is to love God. If you're ever unsure of where to go or what to do, return to this base; everything will flow from there.

Since I became a Christian, I've been in front of tiny crowds and I've been in front of arena-size audiences. I've got to tell you that playing music in front of 15,000 cheering people as a Christian didn't satisfy me. It was very cool, but after I got offstage at my first arena solo concert, I told God that *nothing* I do in this life, not even performing to a full arena crowd, can satisfy me.

Only divine love can truly satisfy me, and my suggestion to you is to get as close as you can to God. Here are a few thoughts about how you can do that:

- Learn how to love God by reading the Bible, which is His love letter to the world.

- Listen to sermons, because faith comes by hearing the word.

- Talk to God like you talk to nobody else—allowing yourself to feel closer to Him than even to a family member, friend, or lover.

- Spend time listening to worship songs and thinking about the love of Christ and everything He's done for you. I'm pretty positive God loves music, and you'll feel His love in its words and melodies if you give Him the time. There are all kinds of worship music available today.

- Go to a church that teaches you how to get filled with the Holy Spirit. It's a great faith-builder.

We're growing in our relationship with Jesus Christ, and it's not always easy. It can be challenging trying to love a God that you can't see. But it's the most awesome challenge that we'll ever have as our faith changes us more and more into the image of Christ Himself.

———

DAY 31

John 20:10-11a (NIV)

Then the disciples went back
to their homes, but Mary stood
outside the tomb crying.

OUR SCRIPTURE PASSAGE for today contains the last two verses that deal with Jesus's death in the Gospel of John. Jesus's followers, reeling from that death, were about to discover that heaven had invaded earth to bring the truth to all the people—including, first, those who were grieving over the death of their Lord.

The truth that it wasn't over. That Jesus was *not* gone forever.

It looked as if Jesus's promised "kingdom" had failed, and Jesus's followers must have been questioning everything He had said to them for those three years they were in ministry together. Imagine what it must have felt like for these people. They'd left their families and jobs to follow Jesus wherever He went. They'd clung to His every word—they'd *believed* Him—and now they were lost without Him. All they could do was just go home or hang out outside His tomb with tears and grief. They didn't have the New Testament like we do. They didn't understand that the story didn't end there.

In the next few verses, though, we see the truth of heaven breaking into the earthly realm. Two angels show up, along with Jesus, to let Mary know that how things *looked* wasn't how things really *were*. It was only a dark cloud making her think that all had been lost. But that cloud would eventually go away. The Light would return. Jesus wasn't going to rot in His grave like other dead people. Nothing could've been further from the truth. He was very much alive and had been given the power to save every single person who walked the face of the earth. Anyone who believed in Him would escape their grave, too.

At first Mary believed only what she saw. Only the shadows of death and lies. But there was a truth that stood firm on the other side of those lies—a truth so resplendent that nobody could have guessed it.

It's the same with our lives today.

I couldn't tell you how many times in my relationship with God things have looked dead and lost, but eventually have turned around. In the beginning of 2008, for example, I lost almost everything, and the people I'd been in business with for years suddenly scattered in the wind. I'd invested so much of myself into everything I did and everyone I knew that I was sick inside, but out of the mess, God brought me to a *way* better place than where I'd been. He gave me a new start with my music that led me to where I am today. Now I'm touring with my new band, traveling around the world. I'm glad I went through that crap—I honestly am—because it taught me the same lesson Mary had to learn: that no matter what things look like, God is in control. God is the master at bringing dead and lost situations back to life. He will fulfill His purpose for my life and yours no matter how things look or feel in the moment. Just think about it: if He can raise people back from the dead, then reviving negative situations must be a piece of cake for Him!

DAY 32

Blessed is the man whose sin the Lord
will never count against him.

HAVE YOU EVER BEEN SO ANGRY that you pierced the heart of someone you loved with the most evil words you could think of?

Unfortunately, most of us learn to hurt with words in one way or another not long after we learn to talk. That's one of the bummers of living in an imperfect world. Where does that desire to pierce others with words come from? Did we get hurt as children? Are we bitter from a former friend or lover who chewed on our heart and spit it out? Are we angry because life has dealt us a bad hand? Or are we just seriously selfish?

Anger is a funny thing. We try desperately to keep it inside, but because we're flawed, sometimes we just have to unleash our anger. Sometimes on a person—usually someone we care about. Sometimes on a thing—an object that just happens to be well placed to receive our anger. Sometimes there's no one around to direct our anger toward, and so we do something far worse.

I know I have—and not just once, either.

One horrible day, back a couple years ago, I felt like I'd turned into a devil. I was boiling over with insanity and wanted to scream at someone to let it all out, but I ended up taking it all out on God.

As I flipped out, I remembered reading in the book of Job that after he'd lost his children and his livelihood, his wife advised him to curse God and die. Luckily, Job wouldn't do it—it seems like one of the worst ways to talk to God—but I remember how filled with hate and rage I was that day. I recall lying on the floor and shouting, "God, I curse you. Now kill me so I can die!"

For some weird reason it felt good to say it.

I'd had so many abusive relationships in my past that when I gave my life to God, I ended up verbally abusing Him, too, whenever I was dealing with massive emotional pain—even though He was all I had. In my past relationships, after I'd hurt the one I loved the guilt would sweep over me and I'd wish I could take my harsh words back. The same thing happened this time with God, but unlike in the other relationships, I was scared that I'd completely blown it with Him, that I'd gone too far. Luckily for me, God will never count outbursts like that against me—not the harsh words, and not the doubt and anger behind them. The people in my past whom I'd verbally abused hung around until they couldn't take it anymore (and I don't blame them for eventually leaving), but God has promised *never* to leave me or abandon me (Hebrews 13:5b). Even in horrible times like those we face daily, God will always love us. He can handle the pain and the cursing.

The point is, since I truly asked for forgiveness for the blasphemous things I'd said, and I've stuck with the Holy Spirit's process of change, God has forgiven and forgotten all of it; He'll *never* count those things against me. It doesn't get any better than that. Jesus was horribly punished in my place. He endured beatings, torture, and crucifixion for my curse against God and for every other horrible thing I've said and done in my life. He did it for you, too. How can anyone not love a person like that? Jesus did everything for you and me, so that we could be made whole. I didn't deserve that, but that's what divine love is all about—a free gift.

I really felt bad about what I said to God that day, but just like every other time that I've screwed up—and there are many!—I felt God pouring His love in me as if to say, "It's okay; I forgive you. You can't help what's inside of you or what comes out. Trust in me to take everything out of you that is not of me. My Son died for every wrong thing you've done or wrong word you've said. Your past, present, and future failures have all been forgiven already. Show me your gratitude by loving me. That's all I ask of you."

You're allowed to make mistakes, so don't be too hard on yourself. You can't change yourself; only God can reach into our lives and change us. He'll do it, too. Next year this time, we won't be where we are today—guaranteed.

DAY 33

Mark 14:22 (CEV)

During the meal Jesus took some bread in his hands. He blessed the bread and broke it. Then he gave it to his disciples and said, "Take this. It is my body."

WRITING OF ANY KIND is not an easy thing, as I'm sure many of you have discovered. Whether it's songs or journal entries or a book, translating thoughts and raw emotions into words takes patience. In the beginning of my first book, *Save Me from Myself,* I mentioned that I didn't really want to write a book because I wasn't very good at writing. I learned quickly that if God calls you to do something, He'll give you the gift to do what He called you to do and put people in your path to help accomplish your goal.

Though it's taken me a while to get used to sharing God through my words, I now see it as an invaluable part of my faith. But like many things, it didn't happen all at once. It took a lot of learning and self-exploration; and despite the practice, even today there are still times when writing leaves me feeling more frustrated than satisfied. I try to motivate myself by remembering that it's something that I've been called to do, but unfortunately even a thought as powerful as that doesn't always do the trick.

During the times that I've struggled with writing, I've come to see that signs often come right before the Holy Spirit enables me to do what I've been called to do. For example, there was one weekend in which I had set aside time to work on this book. I had prayed and felt ready to go. My daughter was staying at a friend's house, so I had all weekend alone to pump out a few pages.

Until . . . I got sick.

Perfect timing.

I tried to write while sick, but I ended up lying around all day, unable to type a thing. At one point that Saturday I told God, "If you want me to write, you'll have to get me motivated"; feeling sick had killed all my motivation entirely. The only thing I wanted was rest. Most of Saturday slipped by and my mind remained blank—that is, until late Saturday night. As I listened to a Christian teaching online surrounding Mark 14:22, the passage jumped out at me. I really felt like there was something in that scripture passage for me.

The Gospel of Mark, chapter 14, is one of the sections in the Bible that a lot of churches use when they pass out Communion; it's the institution of the Lord's Supper. But as with all of scripture, there are other meanings God will show us if we care to ask Him.

God sometimes allows us to be broken like bread and squeezed like a grape so that the Spirit of Jesus can come pouring out of us to bless others. That's what was happening to me that weekend, I believe. I took Saturday off because I felt like crap, but when I woke up Sunday, I suddenly had all kinds of ideas to write about. I believed that God wanted to break me like the bread in Mark 14:22 and share my gift with people:

> He took bread, and after blessing
> it broke it and gave it to them, and
> said, "Take; this is my body."

Because we are Christians, we are all members of the body of Christ. We are all parts made to work as one—*in* One. I was broken and squeezed. If you allow Him, Jesus will bless you, break you, and hand you to others as well, because you are as much a part of the body of Christ as I am. There are no favorites in His body. Our gifts from God are always meant for others. What we get we should always give away.

Whether it's in your faith or in your life, try not to become discouraged if you get stopped in your tracks by something that looks or feels negative. Just ask Jesus to use you and your pain to bless others as he did with the broken bread in Mark 14:22.

Remember: God will never waste your pain. When you're at your weakest is when God's strength comes. What better way to agree with your heavenly Father that He alone is God than to completely trust Him while you allow Him to break you.

DAY 34

Colossians 3:13 (CEV)

Put up with each other, and forgive
anyone who does you wrong, just as
Christ has forgiven you.

WHEN I STARTED going through my difficult financial issues, there were a lot of things I had a chance to think about. I thought about Jennea and whether I was letting her down. I also thought about all the people and companies that weren't getting their money because I wasn't able to pay them what I owed. It didn't make me feel good to know that other people thought I was some kind of flake or idiot with my money (even though I *was* an idiot).

I also thought about the people who had steered me in the wrong direction, toward investments that led me to go broke. Was it their fault I put my trust in their advice? What if there was a reason that my money got mismanaged? A reason that I couldn't see. Had I been thinking badly of the people who'd steered me wrong in the same way that the people I owed money to were now thinking ill of me?

Things like that were good to think about, because they helped shift my perspective from only my point of view. This helped me to forgive people who I felt had taken advantage of me.

The Bible says that before I was ever born, God knew me, and all of the days of my life were written in His book before any one of those days happened (Psalm 139:16). What if I was supposed to walk through all of the money problems as part of my learning process and faith-building? The people I used to be with had talked me into investing in things that were sure—they claimed—to become a success. I was talked into signing personal guarantees at a bank, and I put a good deal of my own money into things, but nothing worked out as promised. Was I angry? Of course! But eventually I saw that there was a learning opportunity in my financial difficulties that was far richer than money. The experience reminded me that it was *eternal* riches I was after—and still am. Not earthly ones anymore.

But man, I can still remember how *stupid* I felt when I realized I'd been screwed over!

I believe that these things were all meant to happen so that I could learn how to live the words I was reading in the Bible and not just leave them in the book when I closed it. I learned how to live out forgiveness with those people who had led me into bad business situations. I forgave them; then I got out of there fast! I literally grabbed my stuff and bailed. We don't ever communicate anymore, but I know that I've forgiven them in my heart.

Opportunities still come into my life to forgive people. It's an ongoing thing. As I already mentioned, when I started touring again, I had to start at the bottom, and starting at the bottom again in the music business meant dealing with some shady people in the clubs. There were definitely promoters who didn't pay us according to the terms of our contract. Some of them even hung out and asked me to sign a bunch of Korn stuff and *then* turned around and stiffed us. One guy just took off, while another bar manager actually shoved one of my guys and told him to leave without the money. That almost turned into a fistfight, but it got broken up before anybody got hurt.

There were even Christian people who didn't pay us. One guy pleaded with us to come and play in his town, guaranteeing us a certain amount of money. When the concert was over, he paid us only a piece of that. He had hoped the money would be there and felt very bad when that wasn't the case— but the end result was that we got stiffed. He didn't even offer to make payments or anything.

Like I said—all *kinds* of opportunities to forgive people!

I know I'm not the only guy who's been ripped off. I've heard many stories about people going through hell before they achieved the success they have today. So, because of the reality of life, I choose to walk the difficult road with the Lord, just as the early Christians did. I want the *real* faith-walk.

Yes, there are all kinds of opportunities to forgive people, and that's the choice I make (even if sometimes a smack in the face seems to make more sense). I *choose* to forgive. The passage for today makes exactly this point. As Christians it's our job to forgive people. Why? Just think of all the stuff the Lord forgives us for. He wants us to forgive people who wrong us just as he forgives us when we wrong him. That's pretty heavy. I've been forgiven for all *kinds* of stuff; how about you? I think we're going to have to ask—and keep on asking—for God's help to forgive people, because I don't believe we can do it on our own. As we saw earlier, we need to learn to "do all things through [Christ] who strengthens [us]" (Philippians 4:13, ESV).

We should choose to use every negative circumstance as a means to get rich in the character and nature of Christ. It won't be easy, but it will bring us closer to Jesus, and at the end of the day, isn't that what we all really want anyway?

DAY 35

Isaiah 66:13a (CEV)

I will comfort you there like a
mother comforting her child.

WHEN I WAS IN THE MIDDLE of my second solo tour in
California, some things went down that shook my life
out of control.

Even earlier, when I'd started the tour, things seemed a
little awkward. I can handle when equipment malfunctions
every once in a while, as it seemed to be doing at the tour's
outset, but when things go wrong *every* show, my two old
enemies Anger and Rage come back into my life uninvited.

Allow me to give you the rundown on what happened:
I was right in the middle of a show when things started to
go very wrong. First, I had guitar problems—the sound was
all wrong and my strap had issues. Then my mic stand kept
moving around, sometimes making me hit my teeth on the
microphone. On top of all that, I couldn't hear anything in
the expensive in-ear monitors I'd purchased just before the
tour started.

All these frustrations came together for me during the
middle of my song "Washed by Blood." The lyrics were

supposed to bring the message of Christ's love, but instead I found myself losing control and freaking out. During the song, I saw a middle finger going up to God—not an imaginary finger, either. It wasn't good, because it was *my* middle finger! I was so freaked—both by the equipment hassles and by my reaction to them—that I messed up the last chorus. That was it: I threw my very expensive microphone down some stairs, stalked off the stage, threw myself into a car, went back to my hotel, and quit the tour.

I stood in my hotel room face-to-face with my enemies Anger and Rage—and then Remorse stepped in. I was completely devastated. I had gone too far, clearly. I had failed . . . again. I agonized over what I'd done for a couple of days. Then a familiar feeling came over me. The Bible says that God will give us peace like a river (Isaiah 66:12), and peace from God to those who are justified by faith in Jesus Christ (Romans 5:1). I learned these truths when I first came to Christ, but sometimes I get so wrapped up in my emotions that I forget.

After God helped me to remember these truths of scripture, my heart burst with the conviction that God was real and was with me. My despair and sadness began to lift. I knew I could go on.

The comfort that God gives to us when our emotions run amok really is like that of a mother comforting her child. We've seen maternal comfort countless times, and most of us have experienced it ourselves. A mother who hears her child screaming runs as fast as she can to get to that child. Her sole desire is to comfort her little one. She holds the child in her arms and gently wipes away the child's tears.

That is a picture of how God comforts us.

The day after I quit my tour, I was angry, guilty, sad, depressed, and confused, but God came to me just when I felt that all was lost. He comforted me and took all the pain away, "like a mother comforting her child" as Isaiah says in our verse. God turned things around so that it was as if my meltdown had never even happened. After a flurry of phone calls to undo the damage I did to the tour, we finished out the last three days of shows, and they were the best shows we'd ever played.

I don't know how He does it, but God always turns the worst days around and makes everything good again . . . every single time.

DAY 36

Acts 20:24 (NIV)

However, I consider my life worth nothing
to me, if only I may finish the race
and complete the task the Lord Jesus
has given me--the task of testifying
to the gospel of God's grace.

LEFT THE SO-CALLED GOOD LIFE. A life filled with beautiful girls, free beer, first-class plane tickets, fast cars, fancy houses, fame, fans—you name it and I had it. It was the ultimate rock star fantasy life that, for some reason, came true for *me*. Ever since I became a rock star, I've had the same questions always come to my mind: "Why was I able to live my rock star dream when so many other musicians in the world who are more talented than I am never get their big break? Why *me* out of so many?" I don't know the answers to those questions, but I do know that after I experienced my rock star dreams to their fullest, I still had profound questions—questions lodged deep in the center of who I was as a person—that I just couldn't let go of.

"Is this all I'm gonna feel in life? Is this all life is about—imagine my dream, strive for my dream, reach my dream, live my dream, make money, raise a family, grow old and then die?"

In other words, is this *it*?

As a kid, I always imagined myself being "complete" when I thought about the possibility of obtaining my dreams, and so my life became a race to acquire as much as I could in this world. I saw fame, possessions, and wealth as the destination. I saw myself totally satisfied with life. I don't know how it happened, but everything that I dreamed about as a kid, and more, came true for me. Yet it didn't take long for those dreams to turn on me. The money and fame that I'd obtained were attracting people who loved just that: my money and fame. They wanted those things more than they wanted me. My music career kept me away from my family, and my creativity as a guitarist slowly died as my drug use escalated. But those questions deep inside of me *still* kept coming up:

"Is this all there is to life? Is this it?"

When God poured His life into me via the gift of His Spirit, those profound questions finally had answers. For the first time in my life, I felt 100 percent complete. I'd been given the answer to what life was all about, and it totally and completely satisfied me. My heart was finally at rest. The feelings I'd received from the gift of faith were enough. They were what I'd been searching for. They were what I'd wanted my rock star dream to make me feel like. They were everything I'd ever wanted out of life.

Finally I was racing to the end with a destination in sight: God's work. For the first time I could *see* my destination, and it was not about cars or houses; it was, as our daily passage says, "the task of testifying to the gospel of God's grace." All my stuff, all my childish dreams—they were nothing compared to God. *My* plans for my life and my dreams were worth nothing to me anymore. It was all about *God's* plans for my life from that moment forward. God is *everything*, and anything less than *everything* just left me wanting more.

My insane mentality used to be, "More money, more fame, more beer, more drugs—more, more, more! Even if it kills me, give me more!" I'm so glad I turned from those things and toward the simple love of Christ. When Christ found me and I believed in Him, my chant became like that of the apostle Paul: "I consider my life worth nothing to me. All I want is to follow Christ—to walk in His footsteps and show everyone how amazing the grace of God is, no matter how unpopular that task is!"

When God introduces you to eternity, your old life will mean nothing to you. All the cares of this world will fade into the background. Why? Because when you have *everything*, you don't want anything else.

Trust me.

DAY 37

2 Corinthians 4:7-10

We now have this light shining in our
hearts, but we ourselves are like fragile
clay jars containing this great treasure.
This makes it clear that our great power
is from God, not from ourselves. We are
pressed on every side by troubles, but we
are not crushed. We are perplexed, but
not driven to despair. We are hunted down,
but never abandoned by God. We get knocked
down, but we are not destroyed. Through
suffering, our bodies continue to share
in the death of Jesus so that the life of
Jesus may also be seen in our bodies.

AS I WRITE THESE WORDS. I'm going through some severe pressure and difficulty.

I'm presently being sued by four different people/
companies for over a quarter of a million dollars, and I also
owe the IRS a huge sum.

But it doesn't end there.

Due to financial difficulties, my house is no longer mine; I was forced to move into an apartment. I've owned nice houses for the past twelve years, so I can't help feeling like a failure in some ways. On top of the negative feelings I have about the whole situation, the apartment managers initially denied my application because my credit was totally screwed up. I ended up having to pay six months in advance in order to move into my new place.

It doesn't end there either. I started a food delivery business with a friend about a year ago. Being a co-owner, I got talked into putting two company vans in my name. When everything fell apart, one of the vans got repossessed, and my BMW will be repossessed next month.

You're probably thinking, "Head, you sold millions of albums with Korn. How can you *possibly* be broke?"

Answer: it's a long story.

In other news, my daughter has a rash all over her body, while her hands and feet are so swollen and painful that she can barely walk. She was diagnosed with laryngitis three weeks ago, and now this. Man, when it rains it pours.

But wait: there's more.

My friend's mom has been in the hospital with major pain for weeks, undergoing tests in hopes of finding out what's wrong. The doctors are stumped. On top of that, my friend's future mother-in-law was diagnosed with cancer a few months ago and is dying a slow, painful death.

I'm also unable to pay any of the new band members I just "hired," but they believe in what I'm doing so much that they're working pretty much on their own dime for now. It's a huge embarrassment for me to tell them that I can't afford to pay them anything after selling over thirty million albums with Korn.

My new bass player, Valentine, rented a car so that he could get around during our band rehearsals. And guess what? Yep, an accident. Another car rammed into his passenger door while he was in a store. Of course, the person was nowhere in sight and nobody saw anything.

You get the idea.

There's so much pressure coming at me from all sides that I feel today's passage from Corinthians on an entirely new level. Some days I feel so much heaviness and negativity from all of life's storms raining on me that I feel like giving up. But I know that's not an option. There's a deposit from heaven that has been placed in the core of my being. I will *never* give up, because the divine guest that lives in me will *never* give up. It's God in me who never quits, and He promises me that when I'm weak and at the end of myself, His power is perfected in me and that's all I need for victory. Period.

It's actually a good sign when things in life come against you as a Christian.

1 Peter 4:12-13 (CEV)

Dear friends, don't be surprised or shocked that you are going through testing that is like walking through fire. Be glad for the chance to suffer as Christ suffered. It will prepare you for even greater happiness when he makes his glorious return.

Believe me, when I'm walking through fire in life, I don't know how to be "glad" as this scripture recommends. But I do know how to be quiet and trust that God will turn everything around. I've seen Him do it too many times to doubt

Him. That's why God allows us to go through fiery trials. The "glorious return" of Jesus that this scripture talks about takes place whenever He comes back to save us from our earthly difficulties—just as He is doing with all my troubles in life. Every difficulty I mentioned earlier has turned around.

Someday Jesus will rescue us from *every* single bad thing in life, but until then Jesus uses trials to make us stronger for the next set of storms that comes our way. He wants to teach us that He is the living Savior who saves us now, not just when we die. But that's part of the reason we grow strong in Christ on earth—so that we will be prepared for our biggest trial: death. Try not to despise your trials. Use them to help make you *stronger*!

DAY 38

Acts 17:28 (NIV)

"For in him we live and move and have our being." As some of your own poets have said, "We are his offspring."

I HAVE HAD SO MANY DAYS where it's felt like God was busy in China or something. When I prayed on days like that, I felt like all I was doing was talking to my walls.

Then one day I was reading my Bible and I found today's verse in the book of Acts. Is it just me, or does this promise that we couldn't get away from God even if we wanted to?

"For in him we live and move and have our being. . . . We are his offspring."

When I think of that first part—"in him we live and move and have our being"—I imagine fish. Yeah, you heard me: fish.

There must be billions of fish swimming in the sea—lots that we know about but many species that have yet to be discovered. They differ in shape, size, and color, but the one thing they have in common is that they need water to live. They can't leave the water; if they did, they would die. Everywhere that fish swim, the water is right there with them and

in them. They can't go anywhere or do anything without the water being completely involved in everything they do.

A similar thing happens with us as we live and breathe on planet earth.

The Spirit of God is often called "living water" (John 4:10). Everywhere we go on earth God is right there with us and in us. He is involved in everything we do. *Nothing* is hidden from God. In Him we truly do live, move, and have our being.

What about being God's "offspring"? Scripture tells us that when we come to Christ, we become children of God. We are spiritually reborn from above with God's nature. God's very own spiritual DNA actually lives within our spirits. I can't tell you how floored I get when I meditate on that. Even knowing the powerful love that I have for my daughter, I find the endless love of God absolutely radical. Jennea makes mistakes just as all children do—as all *adults* do, for that matter. Some are bigger mistakes than others, but the point is, nothing can change the unconditional love that I have for my daughter.

Same with God, but on a bigger scale. We're His offspring. His love for us never fades away. It never stops because we've blown it, though our mistakes just keep coming. In fact, one mind-blowing verse in the book of John says that God actually loves us as much as He loves Jesus (17:23).

Hebrews 4:13 tells us that nothing in all of creation is hidden from God's sight. So if you ever feel like God's busy in China and you're talking to your walls during prayer, as I sometimes do, try to remember what scripture promises in Hebrews and in our focus verse in Acts. It's impossible for God not to see us. He's everywhere. In him we live and move and have our being (remember—the fish!). We are His offspring. We can't go anywhere that God can't see or hear us. It's impossible. Jesus even says that every single hair on our head is numbered. That's how incredibly detailed our brilliant God is.

Meditate on that for a while. God sees all of the things about us and he hears all of our thoughts. If you're anything like me, some of the things you think about could get you thrown in jail if someone read your mind. But one of the coolest things about God is that He loves us *despite* all of the gross inner evil that we try to hide.

That's what unconditional love is all about, my friend.

DAY 39

Romans 8:28 (NASB)

And we know that God causes all
things to work together for good to
those who love God, to those who are
called according to His purpose.

RECENTLY HEARD A TRUE STORY about a guy who experienced a radical change in his life. If you thought *my* life change was amazing, wait until you read this: the guy was a hit man for the Mexican Mafia.

A murderer.

An assassin.

For seventeen years his job was to take people out of this world. That was his duty. If you heard a knock on your door and his face was on the other side when you opened it, that was the last face you would ever see. His whole life was filled with and surrounded by violence. It didn't stop with the violence he directly *caused*, either. His own life was always in danger because of what he did for a living, and he also put his family's lives in danger. Because of his lifestyle, he always expected that he would be killed at a young age.

He eventually ended up serving about five years in prison, having been charged with nineteen counts, including murder for hire and kidnap for ransom. Oddly enough, he beat most of those charges—I guess he had some good lawyers on his side—but he still had to serve time. By the time he got out of prison, he was something of a hero on the streets because he'd done so little time for all his crimes.

But his life as a hero didn't last very long. He got arrested again—one last time.

One last time in the back of a police car. One last time behind bars. Little did he know, his whole life was going to change behind those bars.

After that final arrest he was kept in a high-powered maximum-security prison. I guess being locked up didn't slow down his business any, though, because (while incarcerated) he was actually hired to kill a guy who was serving time in the same prison—coincidentally, in the cell next to his.

One day, as the two men were sitting in their cells, the intended victim called the assassin's name, and they stared at each other via the little mirrors that the prisoners used to see each other. The hit man could see that the guy he'd planned to kill was shooting up dope. As he pumped dope into his arms, he talked to the assassin about Jesus. The assassin got really angry at the mismatch between words and actions and thought to himself, "What a hypocrite!"

The assassin then started to wonder if this guy was just trying to mess with his mind. Suspicious of that, he listened with attention as the intended victim confessed that he was a backslid Christian who still felt Jesus within him. Suddenly, a miracle began to take place: as the assassin listened, the words started to become real to him, and divine love began to enter his heart.

As the assassin's heart was changing, a conflict arose inside. The hit man told his intended victim to shut up because he was starting to cry from what he was feeling inside. He didn't want to cry, but the power of God's love was too strong for the murderer's heart.

One day soon after that experience, the assassin was still trying to decide if he was going to go through with the murder. In the end, he decided he would make the kill after all. He saw the guy in the prison showers later and decided to go for it. He was strapped and ready to kill, while the other guy wore only a towel. But as the seconds ticked by, he found that he just couldn't follow through with the hit. He couldn't kill anymore.

The murderer's heart had been melted by the unconditional love of God. The assassin didn't realize it, but everything in God's world was conspiring to help him find the righteous path. Just like in today's passage, God was causing all things to work together for good through his love.

By the grace and tender mercy of God, that assassin was forgiven, and Jesus made him a brand-new person.

This man, whom God had made a new creation, now travels the world and tells people his story. God caused all things to work together for good in this man, this former killer, because he was called according to God's purpose. He answered that call and allowed God to give him a new heart and a new life.

Some people may wonder, "How can God forgive a killer? What about all those people he murdered? Are they saved, too?"

It's a valid point, but here's the thing: God will take care of all that. Those things aren't for us to figure out; not for us to judge. God sees sin as sin. Stealing condemns us just as severely as an assassin's murder condemns him. But there's *no* condemnation for those who are in Christ (Romans 8:1). I think people should look at it like this: if God loved this murderer and restored his life, then you should be even more convinced that He loves you and will do the same for you.

The hands of God are full of love and mercy, which endures forever. It's a mind-boggling thing that no human being can fathom. Jesus died in place of all of us on earth. Everybody. Even murderers! He chooses people and radically changes them to prove, without a doubt, that he actually exists. That He actually forgives. That He actually saves. Jesus enters those people's hearts and changes their lives. And nobody can explain these transformations.

I believe that God chooses to radically change the lives of people such as this former Mexican Mafia member and a rock star drug addict like me because he wants to show the world the power and the reality of His love. So many people think that people like us are beyond forgiveness, but God has chosen to love us and give us a second chance in life. I think we should all follow God's heart so that we can see this world radically changed. If God could step into this assassin's heart and change Him, He can do it with anybody. It's a spiritual change that no doctor, scientist, or scholar can explain.

Sometimes I wonder if God changes people who are so evil as a way to reach the many people in the world who think they're good enough already—the people who think to themselves, "I don't need to be saved. I've never robbed a bank, killed anybody, or sold drugs. I'm a good person." I believe that *everyone* needs salvation. If you're a human being, you will one day face death, and it says in the Bible that Jesus is the only One who can save you from death. All of us need Christ. Nobody on earth is good enough in God's eyes. That's the whole reason He sent Jesus into the world—to save the world.

There are no other religions that have so many documented radical changes in the hearts and lives of human beings. Those miracles should be all the evidence anybody needs in order to know, without a doubt, that Jesus Christ is the *way,* the *truth,* and the *life* (John 14:6).

DAY 40

2 Timothy 1:6 (CEV)

So I ask you to make full use of the
gift that God gave you when I placed
my hands on you. Use it well.

WE ALL HAVE GOD-GIVEN TALENTS inside of us, waiting to be discovered. Some people know the gift God has given them; some of us don't have a clue. Like me—I didn't have a clue. I was pleased to be good at something when I learned how to play music, but I didn't understand that it was a gift from God. Now that I look back on my life, I see clearly how God worked on my behalf to bring me where I am today. I was chosen, though I don't know why. I'm just really happy about it. And *you* have been chosen, too. I believe this book is in your hands for a reason.

When I first started playing guitar, I took some lessons that were pretty boring. I knew I had to start with the basics, but man, I wanted to be playing my heavy metal, not the boring children's music I was being taught. As a kid, you need to be excited about what you're learning or else it becomes just like school. And most kids are not big fans of school.

Once I got the basic guitar chords down, I started listening closely to my favorite songs and trying to learn them myself. I wasn't perfect at it at first, not by a long shot, but I was making some progress and I was getting excited about it. Some of the things I learned sounded only vaguely similar to the songs I was shooting for, but other times I was spot on. The more I tried to figure out the songs, the more I learned and progressed as a musician. The more I progressed as a musician, the crazier I got about playing music. It was great fun to me!

As I developed my ear to figure out my favorite bands' songs, I soon learned that I could start writing my *own* songs. I called it "making up songs" instead of writing. Reading and writing music always seemed like school activities to me, and I wanted my music to be as far from school as possible.

I wasn't spiritual at all back then, but I was definitely making "full use of the gift" that God gave me—just as it says in 2 Timothy. After a couple years of playing guitar, I'd often jam out with some friends and we'd try to make up our own songs once in a while. We weren't very good at twelve years old, but we did have some decent riffs and it was a blast! As I turned into a teenager, I started getting serious about playing and practicing, because I wanted to do music for a living. I had no other desire for a career than to play music. My dad would talk to me about thinking of other careers that I could fall back on if the music thing didn't work out, but nothing else interested me.

With that goal in mind I knew that I had to get serious about my music. Inspired to discipline myself, I practiced for hours and hours, learning a lot more songs. It was cool when

I got a car at sixteen, because then I could drive home at odd times of the day to practice.

For P.E. class in high school, I was able to take bowling. I'd get up at like 6:30 A.M. and drive to a bowling alley. After class I'd go home and race through a quick breakfast so that I had time to practice my guitar for a little while before I had to go to school. I'd go home again for lunch and practice, and then hit it up after school and at night, too. I was seriously disciplining myself: I wanted to see improvement.

And I did. I would practice playing really fast lead guitar for hours and hours, sometimes amazing myself at how fast and clean I was playing the notes.

When I was seventeen, I started hanging with my girlfriend a lot, but I tried not to let that get in the way of my discipline to practice. My girlfriend and I were into watching soap operas, like *Days of Our Lives*. We would sit there practically all day and watch them, but I always had my acoustic with me on the couch. I'd do finger exercises over and over, as much as I could.

All of that practice was meant to be, because at eighteen, I went through some difficult things that depressed me into putting my music aside for the next few years. My girlfriend dumped me, and my friends who would later become Korn started a new band without me. I was crushed. But because of all the self-discipline, it was as if I'd gone to college for four years and learned my skills really well. By the time the Korn opportunity came up, I was still skilled enough to pick up where I'd left off. I didn't use my talents for God until many years later—you know the story—but everything prepared me for where I am now. And where I am now is where I'm *meant* to be.

Galatians 6:4-5 (THE MESSAGE)

Make a careful exploration of who you are and the work you have been given, and then sink yourself into that. Don't be impressed with yourself. Don't compare yourself with others. Each of you must take responsibility for doing the creative best you can with your own life.

My divine calling in life is to be Brian "Head" Welch, and you have your own calling as well. You are special and unique, and you're *called* to be who you are. God has a specific task for you to do with the gift He's placed inside of you. You may be a songwriter, a skateboarder, a soccer mom, a physician, a customer-service rep, a mechanic, or whatever, but you can—and are instructed to—use your gifts and talents for the Lord.

But the *first* thing God wants is a relationship with you. Everything else will flow once that foundation is laid.

So have fun with God and the gifts He has given you, and remember that your gifts are for you to use in touching other people's lives, not just for yourself.

AFTERWORD

A lot of people don't understand me because I share so much about deep spiritual things. But I have to share the intimate things me and God have experienced together because those very experiences are what made me stronger than I've ever been.

I am a normal, happy, fun person. I love life now, and it's all because God gave me a second chance. When I share my spiritual experiences it releases the miracle to give other people another chance at life, too.

I've seen many things in my life, but seeing people's lives change is the coolest thing ever.

ACKNOWLEDGMENTS

Matt Harper and Adam Palmer—thank you so much for all of your hard work on *Stronger* (as well as my other books). You put so much time into my books, and I just want to thank you for working hard to help get them where they needed to be. They wouldn't be what they are without your amazing gifts.

Joshua Clay—what goes on inside that mind of yours? Ha ha, you brought this book to life with your insane illustrations. Thank you so much for working so fast and meeting the deadlines. You rock, brotha!

God and Jennea . . . I *love* you.

IF YOU ENJOYED THIS BOOK, YOU MIGHT ALSO LOVE THESE TWO BY THE SAME AUTHOR.

AVAILABLE WHEREVER BOOKS ARE SOLD

At HarperOne, our books on spirituality, personal growth,
and religion have changed people's lives,
influenced cultures, and built bridges between faiths.

Visit us online: http://www.harperone.com

Check out our blog: http://goodbooksinbadtimes.wordpress.com/

http://twitter.com/HarperOne — Get your daily tweet fix from us!

http://www.facebook.com/ — Become a fan!

Our http://www.youtube.com/ Channel
A constantly expanding body of video featuring our authors and books

HarperOne
An Imprint of HarperCollins*Publishers*